Teaching Strategies for the College Classroom:

A Collection of Faculty Articles

Edited by Maryellen Weimer, Ph.D.

Foreword by Alice Cassidy, Ph.D.

Published by Magna Publications

Contents

(continued on page 4)

Foreword
by
Alice Cassidy, Ph.D.

When I started teaching university courses, though I enjoyed it very much, I had little guidance on how to do it and few opportunities to talk about it. A few years after I started, when I told a faculty developer about my course, my students, and what I did in class time, she said I was using "think-pair-share," and "jigsaw," and other terms that I had never heard of. The conversation opened my eyes: I hadn't realized that many others were thinking about their teaching and that they have created resources that can be shared.

I used some of these resources to explain to students why some assignments or in-class activities are designed as they are. I expanded my own teaching practice and became a part of the growing community who work on the scholarship of teaching and learning.

We all want to help students and see them succeed, most of us seek practical advice to improve our teaching. This advice can come in many forms. In teaching and learning workshops I've led, I always come away with new ideas from participants. Conversations with colleagues and participating in conference sessions are other good sources of pedagogical guidance.

During my experience at a university-wide teaching support center, I had the pleasure of working with a great many faculty members and others who teach. Their interests and challenges were diverse. Some arrived knowing what they wanted advice on or assistance with and others were less sure what they needed or where to begin. If you came to talk with me about your teaching practice, how would I try to most help you?

I would start with questions to break the ice: In what discipline do you teach? At what level? Are you new to teaching, or have you been doing so for many years? Tell me your class size and make-up in terms of background knowledge, skills and attitudes. Why do you think students are taking your course? Rich information comes out of responses to these questions and can lead to more questions, open discussion and reflection.

This collegial, inquiry-based and conversational approach that I suspect takes place in offices, departments and centers everywhere reminds me a lot of reading an article in The Teaching Professor. The very title of an article draws me in: Yes, I do want to know about warming the climate, daring to be strict, or teaching mindfulness. Yes, I have had challenges with student behavior, and am always keen to hear more ideas on student engagement. The Teaching Professor is really a form of "assistant faculty developer" for me as a teacher.

I cannot overstate the value of learning about the ideas and experiences of colleagues from a variety of disciplines and institutions. It helps your own teaching practice, and it can help you help others who teach. These are the challenges and interests I have found to be among the most common, along with questions I ask or tasks I give to faculty to lead them to a solution:

Course design and syllabus: It's more than the assignments, readings, and class topics. What are the big questions in your field? How would you describe the key goals of the course? What skills, knowledge, and attitudes do you expect students to bring to your class? By the time they have successfully completed the course, what do you want them to be able to do that they probably could not before?

Lesson planning: From the very first class, you have an opportunity to connect with students in meaningful ways. How do you express enthusiasm for the topic? How did you get started in the field? How can you best use the time you have for each class? Think of each class as one important block that is built upon in subsequent classes. How can participatory learning help students achieve the specific objectives for today? How do they, and you, know when that has happened? Have you tried something called a pre- and post-test?

Techniques and strategies for active engagement: Ask yourself what it is that makes it better for your students to spend time with you than for them to simply read the textbook (if there is one) or listen to pre-taped lectures? I am a strong proponent of constructivist theory, where we learn new things by "hanging" or "connecting" them to things we already know.

Assessing student learning: What exactly are you assessing, and how do you express that to students? How will you distinguish between A, B, and C level work? Rubrics help a great deal, one for each assignment and shared with students. How do assignments connect to goals and objectives stated in your course syllabus? How will you help students practice in and out of class time?

Feedback: How and when do you collect these data from students? Is it formative, conducted partway through the course when you can address responses? How do you use summative feedback to revise the course? How might you check in with students "on the fly" during a class, or at the end of it, using it to start the next?

What about in-class peer review? Ask a colleague trained in peer review to meet with you to hear your lesson goals, visit, and take notes; then meet afterward to review. Insight from others can take the form of probing questions that help you see what you didn't before or you knew all along, and this second opinion helps make it real.

Some key points I have learned mirror the philosophy and practice of *The Teaching Professor:*

1. Remember the power of the student voice. Listen to your students. Collect feedback. Ask them about their learning.

2. Talk with colleagues. They may have experienced similar challenges and can help with collective solutions. You are not alone. Work with people in other disciplines. Informal networking events, workshops, and seminars provide new insights to enhance your own practice.

3. Explore the literature on teaching and learning. You might start with a journal devoted to teaching in your own discipline or by exploring how a particular technique is described across various fields.

4. Participate in a conference on teaching and learning. Not only can you share how you help students learn, but you can learn from others, receive valuable feedback, and leave with ideas to try out in your next class.

The end results for you as a teacher are increased confidence, knowledge, and the ability to troubleshoot. The end results for your students are increased enjoyment, appreciation and learning.

May the articles in this collection help you develop your teaching practice. And may you, in turn, become a resource for others.

I am grateful to Dr. Linda Nilson, Office of Teaching Effectiveness and Innovation, Clemson University; Dr. Joanne Fox, Faculty of Science and Dr. Gary Poole, Faculty of Medicine, University of British Columbia for their feedback, which contributed to the development of this piece.

Chapter 1:
The Start of a
Successful Semester

Don't Waste First Days

By Kevin Brown, Lee University, Tennessee

Despite the fact that numerous articles have been written on the importance of the first day, too many of us still use it to do little more than
go over the syllabus and review basic guidelines for the course. This year I
decided to try a different approach, and the results were much more dra-
matic than I expected. I taught real material on the first day. Despite that,
there have been fewer questions about course policies, with some students
actually referencing them without even a mention from me. Let me explain
how I achieved these results.

On the first day (I used this approach in all my courses), I spent the
majority of the time teaching content that related to the overall ideas of the
course. Thus, in Freshman Composition, a course that focuses on experiential learning, I had the students go outside and experience a brief period of
blindness. They took turns taping cotton balls over their eyes and leading
each other around. We then analyzed the experience and talked about how
one might craft a thesis to describe what happened. In a Western literature
class, I introduced the major ideas of the Enlightenment and talked about
how the interplay of reason and emotion would reoccur throughout the
course.

Only after this exposure to course content did I give students a copy of
the syllabus. Rather than going through it in detail, I told students that they
were perfectly capable of reading it. I think we should start assuming that
students in courses ranging from developmental to upper-division major
classes can read and understand a syllabus. Rather than treating the syllabus
as something special, I decided to handle it as another reading assignment.

To prepare students for this reading assignment, I did a brief presentation (I used PowerPoint this year, which I almost never use) on the most important aspects of the syllabus: why students are taking the course, how to
get in touch with me, our university's mission statement, academic support
for those with disabilities, how to access the online readings, and the overall

structure of the class. I limited the presentation to 10 minutes. I have even begun to wonder if I could skip handing out the syllabus altogether and simply have students print it off themselves and read it before coming to the first day of class.

On the second day, I had students pick up note cards as they arrived for class. I asked them to write on the card any questions they had about the syllabus. In one class of just over 30 students, I answered fewer than five questions, and it took less than five minutes. Even in my largest class, which had the most questions, I was still able to respond in less than 10 minutes. Thus, my presentation of the syllabus took 15 minutes at most, as opposed to the 40 to 50 minutes it used to take.

I also used bonus questions taken from the syllabus on my reading quizzes. This makes it clear to students who have not read the syllabus that they are losing out on extra points. I have considered giving a quiz solely on the syllabus, as I have heard some professors do, but that seems a bit petty to me. I can see, though, how that approach reinforces the idea of treating the syllabus as class material, just like any other reading assignment.

In the few weeks since the semester started, I have had more students reference policies from the syllabus than I usually have in an entire semester. Students know how many points I deduct for late papers, and two students in one class wanted to discuss our school's mission statement. They asked if I believed we are actually trying to live it out (we are a religious institution), something that has never happened in my eight years of teaching here.

Rather than wasting that all-important first day going over material students can read on their own, I recommend we begin by introducing students to ideas from the course. Almost all of us complain about running out of time by the end of the semester, but a better beginning can help us reclaim at least one day of it, if we use it wisely.

Reprinted from *The Teaching Professor*, 23.9 (2003): 3.

Ten Things to Make First Day (and Rest) of Semester Successful

By Mary C. Clement, Berry College, Georgia

I like to arrive in the classroom well before the students. It gives me time to get things organized. I create an entrance table (I use chairs or desks if there's no table) that holds handouts for students to pick up. From day one the students learn the routine: they arrive, pick up handouts from the entrance table, and read the screen for instructions. They know what to do, and it saves time. Here's how I recommend introducing the routine on day one:

1. Post your name and the name and section of the class on the screen so that when students walk in they know that they are in the right place.
2. Write "welcome" on the screen and have directions that tell students what they need to do immediately. Example: "As you enter, please tell me your name. Then pick up a syllabus, a card, and a folder from the entrance table. Fold the card so that it will stand on your desk, and write your first name on it in BIG letters. Add your last name and major in smaller print. Write your name on the tab of the folder (last name first, then first name). Read the syllabus until class starts." *Note: By asking students to tell you their name as they enter, you can hear how the name is pronounced and avoid the embarrassment of pronouncing it for the first time yourself.*
3. When it's time for class to start—start class! Late arrivals can catch up by reading the screen.
4. For classes of 25 or fewer, I have students do brief, 10-second introductions. I tell them there will be a verbal quiz after all the introductions and that they can win stars if they know who is who. (Have fun with this, but remember that these are adults and college is not like junior high.)

5. For larger classes, I have students introduce themselves to three or four people around them, and then we might do "stand-ups"—stand up if you are a Spanish major, stand up if you are an education major, and so on. I explain that students need to know each other for our small-group work and in case they have a question.

6. I collect the file folders and put them alphabetically by student name into a big plastic carrying case. When students need to turn in assignments, they find the box on the entrance table, and they put their papers in their respective folders. When papers are graded, they can pull their graded tests or assignments from their folders. The beauty of this system is that time is never wasted by passing out papers. For small classes, I put handouts in the folders of absent students.

7. After the introductions and the explanation of the folder and box system, I turn to the "Today we will" list that I've written on the board, posted on a large paper flip chart, or projected on the screen. I like to actually write this list on the board so I can return to it even while projecting my notes. A Today-we-will list outlines my plan for the day. For example, for the first day, my list says:
   - See screen for instructions for card and folder
   - Introductions
   - Turn in folders
   - Go over syllabus completely
   - Mini-lecture on _____
   - Interest inventory
   - Do you know what to read/do before the next class?

   [Note: The Today-we-will list lets me walk around the room, teach from the projection system, and then look at the list for what I should do next. I tend not to forget things if I have the list. As the semester progresses, the Today-we-will list might contain warm-up questions that then appear as test questions. The list helps students who arrive late or leave early see what they have missed.]

8. For the mini-lesson/mini-lecture—whether it's a short overview of the first reading assignment, some sample problems, or 10 interesting questions students will be able to answer at the end of the course—I strongly recommend doing some course content on the first day. For classes that last longer than 50 minutes, I include a short student activity. I also think it's important to begin with course material on day one so that students begin to see who you are and how you teach. Since I teach courses in teacher education, I often talk about my

teaching career. I include a few stories about how times have changed and about how some things in teaching never change.

9. Interest inventories are great for the first day of class. An interest inventory is just a short list of questions about students' backgrounds and interests. It may assess their prior learning as well. In addition to name and major, students can write about a hobby, interest, or goal. Do not be too personal. You can have them answer several questions about content—maybe solve a problem, write a short paragraph, or answer specific questions. Finally, open-ended questions are useful:

- What are your goals after graduation?
- What has a teacher done in the past that helped you learn _____?
- Is there anything else that you want me to know about you and your course of study?

You can always add one fun question:

- If your song played when you entered the room, what would that song be?

10. Every good class has an introduction, a body, and a conclusion. I usually teach the mini-lesson and then save the last six to eight minutes of class for the interest inventory and individual questions. This way, students don't have to wait on others to finish. I instruct students to turn in their interest inventory as they exit. As they are writing, I alphabetize their folders and put them in the box on the table. Another good closing is to ask whether they know what to read/do before the next class and whether they know three people to ask about the assignment if they have a question.

Reprinted from *The Teaching Professor*, 21.7 (2007): 1.

Critical Connections for First Days of Class

By Joe Kreizinger, Northwest Missouri State University, Missouri

If you typically use most of each opening class session reviewing your course syllabus but seek a more engaging alternative, let me suggest focusing your first lesson on "making connections" rather than "giving directions." The three "critical connections" I emphasize on opening day are (1) **connecting students to instructor**, (2) **connecting instructor to content**, and (3) **connecting content to students**. By focusing on these connections (and saving the syllabus for the second day of class), I aim to create a positive and productive working relationship with my students right from the start and, perhaps most important, to awaken in them early an awareness of the benefits of engaging with the subject matter.

After brief welcomes and opening remarks, I draw three circles on the board and connect them with arrows that suggest a continuous cycle. I write one of the three critical connecters ("me," "you," and "content") in each of the circles. After a brief explanation and preview of the three critical connections, I make an initial personal connection with the class by sharing a bit about myself.

When class size allows, I use a variety of icebreaker activities to connect individual students with one another and with me. I also establish an initial personal connection by collecting information on each student. I distribute a sheet near the end of the first class and ask students to return it next class. It requests basic demographic information but also gives students the opportunity to share more personal information if they choose (e.g., favorites, hobbies, etc.). Using bits of that information later in the course can enhance the personal connections first made during the opening session.

Once I have established this first critical connection (students to instructor), I segue into the second—connecting myself to the content. My primary objectives here are to build credibility, demonstrate interest in and enthusiasm for the content area, and show how the content has been significant to me. I may discuss my research in the area (building credibility) and highlight conferences I've recently attended (showing enthusiasm). I talk about how the content has aided my growth as an educator. I extend beyond my professional life and discuss how this content is useful in my personal life. As an example, in a basic communication course that I teach, I show students how the content may enhance interpersonal relationships, group interactions, and perhaps even self-understanding. I know that most instructors have deep passion for their content areas, but sometimes they fail to communicate that passion in a tangible way. Of the three critical connections I suggest, this one seems to be most often neglected.

By your describing how this content connects with you, it may be easier for students to start to develop similar connections themselves. I don't expect that all my students will find personal relevance on the first day, but you can't expect the connection to develop if it isn't even explored. If students understand how they can make use of the content, they may become better engaged, and I hope they will develop a greater sense of ownership of their education.

In my basic communication course, for instance, I share statistics that illustrate how greatly potential employers value the very communication skills students will be developing in class, and I discuss in very simple terms some of the specific skills we will address and when and where they might be applied in students' personal lives.

I end my opening day by asking students to brainstorm potential benefits that may come from study in the discipline. Following that discussion, I ask each student to write on the back of the "student information sheet" (discussed above) three or more specific ways the content of this course may benefit him or her personally. At the second session, I review some of those benefits.

Even though it takes a bit of time, I have found that placing some emphasis on making connections rather than giving directions on the opening day of class changes student attitudes. They are more positive toward the subject matter and often toward the class in general. Their overall experiences seem to be more productive as well.

Reprinted from *The Teaching Professor*, 20.5 (2006): 1.

'Warming' Climate for Learning

By Sandra Allen, Columbia College Chicago, Illinois

When educators talk about climate, they don't mean global warming. In academic circles, climate refers to the atmosphere of warmth existing between the teacher and the students. Much research suggests that few other factors produce a more lasting impact on learning than the professor's approval or disapproval of the student's work and their in-class interactions.

So, how do we go about climate change? With trial and error and a dollop of research, I've identified three aspects that seem key to creating a "warm" climate for learning: (1) the teacher's praise or approval, (2) enthusiasm for and use of students' own ideas, and (3) teacher-student interaction. To be effective in facilitating student learning, I recommend that we use all three. In fact, praise alone does not definitively correlate with improved student learning.

Praise

Offering praise and approval doesn't mean avoiding messages that let students know when their work doesn't meet acceptable standards. In fact, recent studies show that students want specifics about their performance—not bland, ambiguous feedback, which can actually disrupt student learning. One survey of 100 students found that 70 percent saw their professors as the best source of written or face-to-face feedback on relevant tasks and assignments.

Enthusiasm

In my classroom, I've found that enthusiasm for and use of students' own ideas is contagious. When the teacher gives concrete evidence of valuing a student's diverse approaches—to, say, problem solving—that creates an energy that makes all students more attentive and cooperative. Here are four techniques I use to generate enthusiasm for student ideas. First, acknowledge what students contribute to the discussion.

When appropriate, I point out that their solution to a problem or insight into an issue represents a new twist, maybe even one I have not thought of previously. Second, I modify or rephrase the ideas into concepts that serve as springboards to new material. Next, I compare student ideas by connecting the dots between their thoughts. And finally, I summarize what was said by an individual or a group of students, stating how it applies to the course content.

Another way to more proactively use students' ideas is to solicit their opinions on course content and teaching style. Rare is the student who hesitates to give an opinion anonymously, as those end-of-course comments on rating forms clearly indicate. However, those assessments come after the fact and don't necessarily help the teacher change if the approach in the current course is off. Among the many ways to gather student feedback, the one I prefer is simple, cheap, and easy.

I distribute a three-by-five-inch index card to each student in class a few weeks before midterm. I ask them to write two or three things they have learned so far on one side of the card and to indicate what gets in their way of learning on the other side. After collecting and reviewing this anonymous feedback, I tell students what I learned and what I'm doing (or will do) about it. My response to their feedback lets them know that I value their opinions. I recommend repeating the process again three or so weeks before the final. It's always an enlightening experience to compare the two sets of student responses.

Interaction

Characteristics of successful student-teacher interactions include both verbal techniques that hold student interest and the teacher's physical gestures or movement in the classroom. Being savvy about what's going on verbally and nonverbally with students goes beyond positively responding to student ideas. It gives the teacher the ability to interpret and respond to the classroom dynamic in real time.

Long story short: get out from behind that desk, and move around the room as you talk. Remember: body language is part of a professor's message. Moving among students has the added benefit of identifying those who are busy text messaging and/or using their laptop to refine their lists of friends on Myspace.

It's not a stretch to conclude that a vibrant classroom climate is important to enhancing student attitudes toward the teacher and, by extension, to acquiring the skills and knowledge of the course. Praise by itself might be counterproductive, but it becomes a potent motivational force in the classroom when combined with enthusiasm for student ideas and interaction with the students. Those three together improve teaching and enhance learning outcomes.

Reprinted from *The Teaching Professor,* 22.2 (2008): 1.

Should Students Have a Role in Setting Course Goals?

By Maryellen Weimer, Penn State Berks, Pennsylvania

Maybe ... but then if you ask students what they want to get out of a course, most give the same depressing answer: an A (never mind whether learning accompanies the grade). If you rephrase and ask why students are taking your course, those answers are just as enervating: nothing else was open at the time; it's in the same room as my previous course; my fraternity has copies of your exams on file; my boyfriend's in this class; I heard you were easy; I heard you were funny; your textbook's the cheapest one; or, my favorite on Lucy Benjamin's list, "because my mother took this class from you 24 years ago, and she said I could use her notes." (p. 147)

Do answers like these make those who would give students a role in setting course goals dreamy optimists? Perhaps, but maybe there's another kind of question that we should ask: How did students arrive at this dismal approach to selecting courses? Surely they were not born wanting so little from their education. What experiences could have so disconnected them from classroom learning? Has the educational enterprise somehow disenfranchised them?

Those are large questions, and Benjamin's article does not answer them ... at least not directly. Benjamin's interest is in course goals and the disconnect that exists between the goals of faculty and those of students. Moreover, the goals focused on in the article are not the bogus ones students frequently voice, but rather 17 possible goals for an introductory psychology course (some are relevant to that discipline, most are broadly applicable, and all are listed in the article).

Across the years, Benjamin has given the list to faculty and students, asking each group to identify the three most important ones for an introductory course in psychology. "For college teachers, the most frequently mentioned goal is 11 (content). No other goal achieves anything near the consistency of that selection." (p.147)

Not surprisingly, this number one goal for faculty rarely showed up in the students' top three. They rank highest a goal relating to self-knowledge and understanding, followed by one focusing on the development of study and learning skills and a third highlighting social and interpersonal skills.

Benjamin uses the list of goals on the first day of class. At that time a discussion about teacher goals occurs, as well as some discussion about this research documenting that teachers and students frequently do not share the same goals. This is why students are asked to identify their top three goals. The results are shared in the following class session.

Benjamin discusses three ways of responding to student goals. First, take a totally student-centered approach and adopt those goals for the course. This approach is not recommended. Second possibility: compare student and faculty goals and then show students why/how faculty goals are superior. No recommendation here either—why seek input if you have no intention of responding to it?

Benjamin's choice is the third option, in which faculty and student goals are integrated. "Do not misunderstand this compromise strategy. It is not meant to undermine the professor's goals, nor is it meant to give students the impression that their goals will become part of the course when there is no intention on the part of the instructor to do so. ... The purpose of involving students in the process is to create a course that is more meaningful to students and professor, to increase the satisfaction of all involved in the class on both sides of the lectern, and to show students how important it is to become involved in their learning." (p. 148)

The rest of the article then explains how Benjamin incorporates student goals into the course. From work attempting to do this, Benjamin has discovered that most often this does not involve changing course content. "More commonly ... meeting student goals is about making specific linkages between what you teach and how it relates to student goals." (p. 149)

Could it be that students take courses for poor reasons because their goals have been ignored or thoroughly sublimated to those more important instructor goals? It's an interesting question and one that can be pursued pragmatically by using (or revising) the list of course goals contained in this article. It might at least be worth a conversation with students.

Reference: Benjamin, Jr., L.T. (2005). "Setting course goals: Privileges and responsibilities in a world of ideas." *Teaching of Psychology*, 32 (3), 149.

Reprinted from *The Teaching Professor*, 20.10 (2006): 8.

Making Syllabus More than Contract

By Roxanne Cullen, Ferris State University, Michigan

For years I've introduced my course syllabus by saying, "This is your contract for the course." And all too often the document read more like a contract than a true representation of my conceptualization of the course.

So I revised my introductory composition course syllabus in an attempt to create a more learner-centered academic experience. Although these elements have been at the core of my teaching, my syllabus did not necessarily make them explicit or clearly articulate their function to the students. Based on advice I found in several resources regarding the syllabus, I came to see that a teacher needs to consider the ways a syllabus can be useful to students. My goal was to make my syllabus more than the standard contract between my students and me. I wanted it to become a tool for learning.

I began by analyzing my syllabus using a rubric that I developed with a colleague based upon principles of learner-centered pedagogy. The original design of the rubric was as a tool for administrators to determine the degree of learner-centeredness in a department or unit based upon a review of course syllabi. In this case I simply applied the rubric to my own syllabus.

The rubric has three main categories, each with several subcategories. The main category, **Community,** includes subcategories that relate to the accessibility of the teacher, the presence of learning rationale, and evidence of collaboration. In the category **Power and Control**, the subcategories focus on teacher role and student role, use of outside resources, and the general focus of the syllabus: Does it focus on policies and procedures, or is it weighted toward student learning outcomes? Is there opportunity for negotiation of policies, procedures, assignment choice, and the like? And finally, in the category **Evaluation and Assessment**, the subcategories examine the use of grades, the feedback mechanisms employed, types of evaluation, learning outcomes, and opportunities for revising or redoing assignments.

A review of my syllabus inspired me to revise. I made several changes to emphasize the concept of community. Although I have always provided rationales for assignments when I talked about them in class, I added a rationale statement for assignments in the syllabus. I also provided rationales for all policies and procedures so that they would look less like arbitrary laws set down by the teacher and more as though they served enhanced learning.

I also incorporated more teamwork and collaborative projects, again with a rationale tied to learning outcomes. Finally, I made an effort throughout to disclose information about myself, mostly in regard to my experience as a composition teacher and a writer.

The most significant change I made was in the area of power and control. Instead of establishing an attendance policy, class participation rules, or penalties for late work, I indicated that all these would be negotiated by the class. Because the course is populated by first-semester students, I was reluctant to share much more power than that, knowing the propensity of beginning students to underestimate the challenge of college-level work.

My former one-page syllabus was now 10 pages and included a short philosophical statement on learning to write along with writing- and learning-related justifications for every policy and procedure. After all this time and effort, I couldn't bear the thought that students would not read it or would simply listen to me ramble through it the first day of class and then never look at it again.

So, in an effort to make the syllabus a working part of the course in which students discovered for themselves what they needed to know about the course, I had them write their first essay on the syllabus. I asked them to consider things such as their expectations of the class, what they thought my expectations were, what they thought they knew about me, and what their roles and responsibilities included.

I was actually eager to read the essays. In some respects, I felt that my work was being evaluated by the students, which provided an interesting twist on power and control. Their essays became another feedback mechanism for me. Equally if not more interesting was the conversation among the students as they prepared to write. I use WebCT, so I suggested to students that they use the discussion board tool as a prewriting strategy.

The discussion was lively and, I believe, productive. Even students who had been reluctant to participate in class discussions about the syllabus weighed in online with great authority regarding their interpretation of it.

Every syllabus is in some respects a reaction to the previous semester, so like all syllabi, mine is still a work in progress. Most important at this point is the tone my new syllabus has set for the semester.

Making the first essay a response to the syllabus has focused more thought and time on it than in any of my previous classes. It has served as a catalyst for discussion, for setting goals, and for discussing writing. It has focused our attention on learning and made every aspect of the course intentional. This syllabus is much more than the standard contract between my students and me.

Reprinted from *The Teaching Professor,* 21.9 (2007): 5.

Establishing Relevance

By Jeff Fox, Brigham Young University, Utah

Students frequently wonder and sometimes ask "Why are we doing this? Why do I need to know this? Why are we spending so much time on this? Why do we have to do this busywork?"

When students don't see the connection between the content and activities of the course and their future lives, they question what's happening and what we ask them to do. Research confirms that perceived relevance is a critical factor in maintaining student interest and motivation. It also contributes to higher student ratings on course evaluations.

Three straightforward practices can help faculty establish the relevance of course content and activities: faculty should (1) regularly share and discuss the learning outcomes of the course; (2) clearly tie those learning outcomes to the required activities and assignments; and (3) orient students at the beginning of each class period by discussing the "what, why, and how" of that day.

Learning outcomes—in the syllabus and during class discussions. Clear learning outcomes are the foundation of a learning-centered syllabus and a basic tenet of all instructional design. Many faculty (perhaps with "encouragement" from accreditation commissions) now include course learning outcomes in their syllabi. If you don't, consider doing so. Outcomes help clarify what students will know and do when they complete the course.

Moreover, faculty should do more than just list the learning outcomes. They should also clearly and frequently discuss the relevance of the outcomes with students. Students need to know why the knowledge and skills identified in the learning outcomes are important in their future lives. We know that the content is relevant, but we shouldn't assume students see how it relates to what they will be doing.

Link assignment descriptions and learning outcomes. Most faculty do not regularly tie the assignments described in the syllabus to the learning outcomes. Faculty may think that the links are obvious to students, but that's not always a valid assumption. Every assignment should be clearly defined in terms of how it should be done, and each assignment should be clearly justified by answering questions such as "How does this assignment relate to the course outcomes? How will this assignment help fulfill them? What should the student be able to know or do better after completing the assignment? Why was this assignment chosen to achieve the learning outcomes?"

For example, I explain to students how the assignments are tied to the learning outcomes and how I designed each assignment to exercise different intellectual skills in Bloom's Taxonomy. When students understand what the assignments are helping them accomplish, they see the assignments' utility and find the work more meaningful.

Establish relevance at the start of every class period. Some faculty members present an outline of the day's material on the board or in a PowerPoint. This is a useful practice that can aid student note taking, but students are even more motivated when the day's content and activities are placed in the context of the course and their lives. Kicking off class with a simple orientation that answers three questions—what? why? and how?—can get students on track, motivate them, and help them put the day's content and activities into context.

- **What?** What are we doing in class today? What questions will we try to answer? What concepts will we address? What questions will we answer? What activities will we do?
- **Why?** Why are we studying this? How are today's content and activities tied to the course learning outcomes? What should I know or be able to do after today's class? How can the information and skills be used in everyday life?
- **How?** How are we going to address the content? Will we use lectures? Activities? Discussions? How will different learning styles be accommodated?

When students understand clearly the value, purpose, and procedures for course activities and the logic by which teachers arrived at their design, they are more likely to see the value of what they are being asked to learn and consequently will participate more fully in the course.

Reprinted from The Teaching Professor, 25.5 (2011): 1.

What Influences Student Attitudes toward Courses?

By Maryellen Weimer, Penn State Berks, Pennsylvania

The first and most obvious answer is the instructor. Much previous research establishes the powerful ways instructors influence how students respond to and in a course. But two researchers wondered whether the instructor was the only factor influencing student attitudes. Drawing from work in their discipline, services marketing and management, they extrapolated seven factors that might be significant determinants of student attitudes. Using a complex statistical model, they tested the seven factors and found that four of them explained 77 percent of the variations in attitude toward the course: instructor, course topic, course execution, and the room (physical environment).

They write of these findings: "An important result is that there are significant factors, in addition to the instructor, at work shaping a student's attitude toward a class that he or she may take. The model shows that course topic has just as strong an influence on attitudes as does the instructor." (p. 144) Only required courses were included in the study. They covered topics about which students had a range of interest, from not being interested at all to the course topic being introductory to a major.

The researchers point out that if the subject matter of a course influences how students relate to a course, then their level of interest ought to be acknowledged as a contributing factor on course evaluations. At this time most course evaluations focus exclusively on instructor-related variables.

Equally interesting in this work are those other factors **not** found to influence student attitudes toward courses. For example, the student him- or herself was not found to significantly contribute toward attitude about the course. The researchers explain why they were surprised by this finding. "Given the emphasis some educators place on encouraging students to take ownership of their education, it was surprising to find that, overall, this group of students did not see themselves as being instrumental in shaping their own education experience." (p. 146)

What the findings confirm is that students (at least those in this cohort) do not understand that they are at least partially responsible for what happens to them in courses. It seems to reconfirm the extremely passive orientation many students have toward knowledge acquisition.

Also surprising was the fact that other students were not seen as a factor influencing student attitudes. This means that "educators cannot assume that students will automatically appreciate the value of the diverse student population that takes a given college course together." (p. 146)

Finally, in a follow-up analysis that explored some of the factors related to course execution (which these researchers defined as overall design and conduct of the course), there was confirmation for some facts about participation many of us have observed in our individual classrooms. "Students in classes where participation was expected and graded were significantly more likely to prepare for class, attend class, and commit to excellence. Students in those classes where participation was emphasized were also significantly more likely to value the contributions that other students make to their learning experiences." (p. 146)

Reference: Curran, J.M., and Rosen, D.E. (2006). "Student attitudes toward college courses: An examination of influences and intentions." Journal of Marketing Education, 28 (2), 135–148.

Reprinted from The Teaching Professor, 20.10(2006): 4.

Chapter 2:
Building Rapport
with Students

Rapport:
Why Having It Makes a Difference

By Maryellen Weimer, Penn State Berks, Pennsylvania

Rapport, defined as "the ability to maintain harmonious relationships based on affinity" (a definition cited in the article referenced below), is more colloquially thought of as what happens when two people "click"—they connect, interact well, and respond to each other favorably. Often it happens when two people are very much alike or have lots in common.

That's one of the reasons it isn't always easy for professors to establish rapport with students—sometimes there's a big age difference; other times it's having few (if any) shared interests.

However, there are good reasons for faculty to work on establishing rapport with students. The article referenced below lists outcomes, all established by research, that result when rapport is established. Not all of the research cited involves higher education classrooms, but here's a selection from the larger list that does seem particularly relevant and that is supported by some research involving teachers and students:

- **Higher motivation**—When students feel rapport with their teachers and feel that their teachers' personalities are something like their own, motivation is higher.
- **Increased comfort**—When there is rapport, students tend to answer more freely and with a greater degree of frankness.
- **Increased quality**—In a degree program, when students feel rapport with faculty, their perceptions of the quality of that program increase.
- **Satisfaction**—Rapport leads to satisfaction; this is supported by much research, including research done in classrooms. When students report having rapport with the instructor, their satisfaction with the course increases.
- **Enhanced communication**—As rapport grows, so do understanding

and comprehension. Teachers and students understand each other better when there is rapport between them.

- **Trust**—Sometimes trust is necessary for rapport to develop. But trust can also be an outcome. Once rapport has been established, trust between parties grows.

What's missing from the list is learning. Rapport does not result in learning, but it certainly helps create conditions conducive to learning—things such as higher motivation, increased comfort, and enhanced communication. Teaching doesn't always result in learning either, but, like rapport, it is one of those factors that can contribute positively to learning.

The researchers in this article queried business faculty about their perceptions of rapport—what must a teacher do to establish it with students? Five factors appeared almost twice as often as others.

Respect. Teachers and students must show respect for each other, for the learning process, and for the institution where it is occurring.

Approachability. Students have to feel comfortable coming to faculty, and faculty must be willing to speak with students after class, during office hours, via email, and on campus.

Open communication. (This dovetails with approachability.) Faculty must be honest. There needs to be consistency between what faculty say and what they do.

Caring. Faculty must care about students; they must see and respond to them as individuals. They also need to care about learning and show that they want students to learn the material.

Positive attitude. Faculty should have a sense of humor and be open to points of view other than their own.

Like many other aspects of effective instruction, rapport is not something developed by announcement. You don't get it by saying you'd like to have it. Rapport is developed by actions—it results from things teachers do. The good news, as demonstrated by the content of this article, is that we know empirically what teachers can do to establish rapport. The even better news is that the actions required aren't all that difficult to execute.

Reference: Granitz, N.A., Koernig, S.K., and Harich, K.R. (2009). "Now it's personal: Antecedents and outcomes of rapport between business faculty and their students." *Journal of Marketing Education*, 31 (1), 52–65.

Reprinted from *The Teaching Professor*, 21.6 (2007): 2.

Getting to Know You: Importance of Establishing Relationships

By Patricia Kohler-Evans, University of Central Arkansas, Arkansas

About two or three semesters ago, I conducted an informal experiment with two of my classes. With one, on the first night of class I asked students their names and major courses of study. I introduced myself in much the same way, with a brief statement about my chosen field. With the other class, I spent time during the first and second class sessions on activities designed to acquaint students with each other and establish how we would conduct the class. I used what I learned about students that first night throughout the rest of the course.

When I compared feedback from the two classes, I was amazed at the differences between the two. For example, one student from the second class noted that these activities made the class more "user friendly." He left class looking forward to the rest of the semester.

I'd like to share some of the activities I used to get students connected with each other and with me.

What's in a name?

When students introduce themselves, I ask them to tell us their name and also to share what that name means, if they know that; to talk about the individual for whom they were named; and to indicate whether or not they like their name. I have also asked whether they live their name. For instance, my name, "Patricia," means loyal. I tell students that fits because I am generally a faithful friend. In some cases students don't know what their name means. I have found that they are very willing to do some research to find out what it means and to then share that information with the rest of the class.

T-shirt collage

Sometimes I have students introduce themselves to each other by creating a T-shirt that represents who they are. I supply each student with a pre-drawn T-shirt pattern on a sheet of paper. I ask students to use magazine pictures, markers, crayons, and the like to design the shirt.

Usually, I bring all the materials to class. Students tend to talk to each other about themselves as they are designing their T-shirts. I do a shirt too. I believe this shows students that I value this activity. Students seem to really enjoy doing this activity, and they usually work very hard to include multiple aspects of themselves in the collage. Students listen attentively when it's time to share the T-shirt collages, and even at the end of the semester they still remember information about their classmates.

Identification of personal interests

In many of my classes, I ask students to share information about their personal interests and learning preferences. I use a questionnaire to obtain this information, and I tell students to share only what they are comfortable having me know. A commercially available product that generates this information is the Learning Express-ways™ folder. (Published by Edge Enterprises, 708 W. 9th St., Suite 107, Lawrence, KS 66044. Phone: 785-749-1743. Fax: 785-749-0207.)

Asking for written feedback

I frequently ask for written comments at the end of lectures. Students may comment about the class, express a concern, or share other information. I respond to all comments in writing and return them at the next class. Sometimes I ask students to rate their understanding on a 1-to-10 scale, and sometimes I ask for a brief reflection.

Since I have started to invest more time in getting to know my students, I have noticed that my relationships with them have improved in numerous ways. When students come to me after the course has ended, I still remember their names and something about them.

I have also noticed that I have more students asking questions about their chosen fields. They regularly tell me that they value the activities as well. I believe that the time invested in relationship building increases students' motivation and commitment to the course.

Recently, I overheard one student commenting to another about a group assignment that I had made. She was admonishing her fellow classmate to seek out other students who were different as a way to enrich the experience. Whether these examples are a direct result of the relationship building I can't say for sure, but I am convinced that it does make a better climate for learning in my classes.

Reprinted from *The Teaching Professor,* 21.8 (2007): 4.

Good Teaching as Vulnerable Teaching

By Rob Dornsife, Creighton University, Nebraska

I was recently asked by a friend and colleague to review her syllabus. She wanted to make sure she had enough policies to address all the classroom issues that now emerge. Policies regarding plagiarism, class cancellation procedures, references to various official university handbook codes, and even mandated contingencies for an H1N1 virus outbreak were dutifully laid out. Indeed, the syllabus, despite some mention of the course itself, read far more like a legal document than an introduction and a guide to a classroom experience.

My colleague reported that this is what she had been told to include on the syllabus, and she was anxious to do what was expected. Still, I sensed she was not totally comfortable with what her syllabus had become. For example, her section on the college's process for handling plagiarism was itself twice as long as her succinct description of the actual course material and how the students might be expected to engage in it—in this case in a terrific assignment sequence geared around eco-critical thinking, writing, and awareness.

As I listened to her struggle to explain and justify the various policies, I began asking questions, gently and in good humor, about the loopholes— the ones that in my experience some students have keen ways of navigating to their perceived advantage. Was a roommate's grandmother's recurrent illness a "genuine emergency"? What constituted an "outbreak" of a virus? Were all students who appear to have cheated to be treated identically and absolutely? It quickly became clear that while fair policies are desirable and necessary, no policy can address any and all eventualities, and none are immune to student attempts at circumvention.

"So, what do we do?" my colleague asked. Even though I've struggled with these issues, I was a bit surprised by the first response that came to me.

"We need to remain vulnerable, and we need to celebrate our vulnerabilities as teachers."

Now that I've had a bit of time to reflect, I've decided that it was a good response. If I am not willing to be vulnerable with my students, I am not able to teach them. There are risks here—and not just a few and not just those associated with our policies and their loopholes. Being vulnerable is the inevitable result of the trust we must have in our students as we expect to teach and learn from them and with them in every respect.

I recently had a student who was missing classes and not submitting work. In a supportive spirit, I invited him for a talk. I explained that I really wanted to help him pass the course. Surprised that his performance was in such peril, he replied that he needed to pass the course—he was graduating that semester. Then he explained that he had just been diagnosed with cancer.

Now I was really concerned and shaken. We, of course, stopped talking about course-related concerns and discussed his prognosis, his fears, his challenges, and the like. My student did not yet know too many details. That evening I called a friend who had won a battle with the same cancer and spoke with him at length, taking notes about the options under various circumstances and so forth.

The next day on my way to class, I saw at a distance my cancer-stricken student, walking happily and joking with his friends. Soon he came to my office to discuss makeup work and so forth. I readily accommodated his requests. When I mentioned that I had talked at length with a friend who had a similar diagnosis, my student appeared sheepish and said he had to hurry or he'd be late for class. Not wanting to impose, I told him I was always available and that I hoped to see him soon.

He got the makeup work done. Considering his stress, his performance in the class was admirable: he more than passed the course. I distributed his final grade sheet last, hoping that would give me a chance to inquire about how he was doing. It was then, more sheepish than ever, that he informed me that he had been misdiagnosed and was in fact fine after all.

I'll let you draw your own conclusions about what happened in this case.

But the more important question is this: Would you as a teacher do anything differently if faced with a similar situation down the road?

I have affirmed that I would not. The benefits of being vulnerable as a teacher far outweigh the risks.

I need my students to know that I care about what we are working on together, and thus I care about them, even though I risk being taken advantage of. I want them to take risks when they approach learning new material, and to encourage them I need to model such risk-taking myself, even as it leaves me open to criticism.

No syllabus can ever make the classroom totally safe for teachers, and maybe we should not be so invested in trying to make it so. Ultimately, for every student who negatively takes advantage of our openness, there will be scores more who thrive because of it.

I have long argued that our students need not "like" us, except to the extent that their affection facilitates their trust in us. I also believe that students do not resent it when we challenge them with higher expectations, as long as they trust that we are fair and open. And in order for them to trust me, I must trust them—as foolish as I may, or may not, appear when I am duped.

Because far more often than not, vulnerability provides what's necessary for teachers and students to excel.

Reprinted from *The Teaching Professor,* 26.10 (2012): 1.

Dare to Be Strict

By Joseph W. Trefzger, Illinois State University, Illinois

In "Good Teaching as Vulnerable Teaching" (*The Teaching Professor*, December 2012), Rob Dornsife of Creighton University invites us to embrace the uncertainties teachers encounter. The article prompted me to invite colleagues also to embrace being strict when the conditions warrant it.

For two decades I have taught 150- to 200-student sections of Introductory Financial Management to majors in all business programs plus business minors from diverse fields. Although the course has its fans—some even change their majors to finance each semester—many students find the material daunting, become distracted, and behave in ways that impede the learning of others along with their own. Distractions always have lurked in college classrooms; texters and Web surfers are merely the note passers and campus newspaper readers of the digital age.

My syllabus, therefore, stresses the expectation that those enrolled will attend class regularly; remain attentive; and refrain from conversing, napping, or doing things unrelated to what we are discussing. I am convinced that most students support these policies based on the many who have thanked me over the years for making classroom order a priority.

They report that some instructors do not admonish disruptors, leaving frustrated victims to bear that awkward task themselves or to suffer silently. It makes sense that serious students would endorse these guidelines. What might be surprising are examples of reactions from some of the offenders whom I've confronted.

Three students, assigned to adjacent chairs by an alphabetical seating chart, chatted incessantly at the start of a new semester. When numerous polite warnings proved futile, I announced in class that we would be switching the trio to new seats. Two from the group were contrite when we spoke after class, but agitated "Larry" asserted loudly and repeatedly that I was "unprofessional" and had embarrassed him in front of friends. (He was unmoved by my response that he had embarrassed me by ignoring my requests.) After venting for several minutes, he left but returned next session and remained grudgingly cooperative for the rest of the course.

Fast-forward four years: quiet and diligent "Lenny," Larry's lookalike sibling, was on my roster. Later, at a homecoming event, Larry spotted me; he shouted my name and bounded over with his hand extended as though we were long-lost pals. He talked about his job and a recent promotion. I mentioned that his younger brother had been in my class. Larry explained, "Yeah, I told him to take your section; you don't put up with crap from people who are there to play around."

Intellectually capable "Matt" did not cause problems directly, but he seldom attended and was inattentive when present, content to waste opportunities and slide by with middling grades. Seeing him in the hallway, I would comment on his indifference. When he stopped by the office just before finals week, I thought he hoped to ask questions about what he'd missed.

However, instead he was there to tell me "I really like how you handle the class." Suspecting it was a snow job to curry favor, I suggested he had no clue what I did because he was rarely in class. But he continued that, as an education major, he took notice of instructors' techniques. "Next year I'll have high school students, and I'll speak up like you do when they don't give their best effort. They need to hear that you want everyone to learn."

Finally, "Kerri" attended infrequently, submitted no homework, flunked tests, and ended the term with an F. When she enrolled next semester, I assumed that she had seen the light and would be responsible in her second attempt. But she skipped classes and badly failed the first exam. So I emailed, "Why are you treating my course like a joke again?" She meekly answered, "How do you even know who I am?"

I wrote that I remembered talking with her the prior semester and was wondering why she was jeopardizing her degree with the same foolish approach. She replied, "I am sitting here crying. I did not realize that a teacher in a class that big would care about one person." Kerri changed into an exemplary student with perfect attendance and solid B work from that point on. She has stayed in touch with me since graduating.

Even students who seem to disregard our directives can appreciate their intent. Indeed the evaders typically mean no grave harm, often just needing guidance and encouragement. And while calling out a violator never is pleasant, it is necessary to bite visibly at times if our barks are to be heeded.

Sustaining an environment conducive to learning is an obligation we owe to committed learners. Some strict rules designed to address specific concerns, applied impartially and consistently, can reward students' more productive inclinations and help us convey what experience tells us is required for academic success.

Reprinted from *The Teaching Professor,* 27.2 (2013): 3.

How Much Control
for How Much Learning?

By Maryellen Weimer, Penn State Berks, Pennsylvania

For quite some time now I've been interested in a widely held set of assumptions faculty make about the need to assert control at the beginning of a course. The argument goes something like this: When a course starts, the teacher needs to set the rules and clearly establish who's in charge. If the course goes well, meaning students abide by the rules and do not challenge the teacher's authority, then the teacher can gradually ease up and be a bit looser about the rules.

The rationale behind this approach rests on the assumption that if a teacher loses control of a class, it is very hard to regain the upper hand. In these cases, student behaviors have compromised the climate for learning so seriously that the teacher has an ethical responsibility to intervene and reassert control.

But these examples are also extreme and, in my experience, rare. Far more common are classroom environments where the teacher is so in control that students passively perform what look like learning tasks (taking notes, feigning attention, etc.).

Lately I've been wondering how much control is necessary to set the conditions for learning and whether that amount of control needs to be offset by a certain amount of freedom so that students can make the learning experience meaningful to them. And then there's the question of how teacher control affects the motivation to learn. Do students learn more or learn better in classrooms that are rule-bound?

More fundamentally, I've been wondering whether those assumptions about needing to establish control at the outset are supported by evidence, experiential or otherwise. What happens if you don't? Do students automatically rise up and take control? Why do I have such trouble imagining students doing that? They seem so beaten down already.

More sinister are questions of whether teachers benefit more from the control they assert than students do, even though most faculty members I know would go to their graves arguing that they control only for the students' sake. A tightly controlled classroom environment certainly makes for safer, saner teaching.

If all potential challenges to authority are headed off at the pass, then the teacher can devote full attention to the content, and isn't that where the teacher's expertise really shines? And so the classroom becomes a place that showcases teaching more than learning?

My suspicion is that most teachers overreact to potential threats. Why? Do they question whether they can respond successfully to challenges? Are they in denial about the vulnerabilities that are inherently a part of teaching? Do they like this feeling of control? Depending on the teacher, all these answers may be possibilities, but I think for more teachers, it's a matter of not trusting students or having lost faith in all of them because of the actions of a few.

It is true that students unused to the rigors of college learning look for the loopholes. They opt for the easy way—so if the teacher stands idly by, they will not demand much of themselves or of their classmates. Most of today's college students aren't going to do well in an environment where there are no rules, little structure, and low expectations, but the question is how much do they and their teachers need, and how is the learning environment compromised when teachers err on the side of rigid control?

Reprinted from *The Teaching Professor*, 22.3 (2008): 4.

Friendly, but Not Their Friend

By Mary Clement and Katherine Whatley, Berry College, Georgia

Today's college instructors are expected not only to be engaging in their classes but also to engage students outside the classroom. Whether it's supervising service-learning, taking students to professional conferences, leading study sessions in coffee houses, or inviting students into our homes, faculty are now expected to be with students in ways that change the kinds of relationships teachers and students have in the classroom.

Teachers now interact with their students in a variety of contexts, many of them informal and some of them purely social. These new roles blur the line between being friendly toward students and being a friend of students. This matters whether you've been teaching for a while and no longer look like a student or your academic career is just starting. All faculty need to know how to build supportive and positive but businesslike relationships with students.

What are some strategies for developing the right balance between being friendly with students while still being their professor? They start with building respectful relationships. How the instructor asks and answers questions adds to the development of friendly yet respectful relationships.

In her book *Teaching Your First College Class,* Carolyn Lieberg (2008) writes, "All of us feel cared about when people look at us when we speak and truly listen to our ideas or questions. Students also feel cared about if you show that you are accessible to them outside of class. ... The basic message is that students want to be treated with respect." (p. 11) Inside or outside the classroom, our interpersonal communication should be built on respectful exchanges.

Sometimes actions that seem unimportant help establish these respectful relationships. Professional attire is a good example. Even though professors don't teach in academic regalia anymore, it is still appropriate to dress more like a professional and less like a student. Faculty who look like students can expect students to respond to them as if they are students. Professional language is also a must. It is another way that professors differentiate themselves from students, and in most professional contexts four-letter words are not appropriate.

When we leave the classroom, the norms change in small but significant ways. It is important to keep the right professional distance, whether meeting with students in your office or having them in your home. The age-old advice of keeping your office door open at all times when you are meeting with students is as relevant today as it always has been.

If students are joining you in your home for a study session or end-of-semester gathering, make sure that you have another "adult" in the home (your spouse, a trusted friend, or another professor). It is not a good idea to have a student arrive early to help organize the event or to have one stay late to help clean up.

The question of whether or not to serve alcohol depends on several factors, including the campus culture and the legal drinking age of the students. It is never a good idea to serve alcohol to undergraduates, even if they are of age, if they must drive home.

What about the distance between you and students electronically, whether it's email or social media? Should the professor "friend" his or her students as a means of communication? Are Facebook and LinkedIn viable ways to reach students and further help them learn? How informal should emails and Twitter messages be?

Rather than answer these questions, we pose them for your discussion. Creating a social media site specifically for class interaction is quite different from friending your students on a personal site. It is good to always remember that all electronic communications can go public at any time. Nothing is confidential.

How friendly should a professor be? Consider a parallel to the old Golden Rule. When interacting with students, ask yourself, "As a student, how would I feel if my professor made this request of me or responded to my question this way?" Those of us with children can ask the question another way: "How would I feel if my son or daughter's college instructor did this?"

The question can be asked more bluntly: "Could this interaction be defended before parents and administration?" And perhaps the toughest version of all: "If this interaction were quoted on the front page of the local paper, how would it appear?" With those questions guiding your decision making and some old-fashioned common sense, you can have productive, engaging, and friendly relationships with your students.

Reprinted from *The Teaching Professor,* 26.5 (2012): 4.

Caring for Students:
How Important Is It?

By Maryellen Weimer, Penn State Berks, Pennsylvania

Most teachers know that caring for students is important, but do they realize just how important? A recent article by Steven A. Meyers offers a succinct, well-referenced, and persuasive review of research that addresses the topic. It begins with what most teachers already know: caring is regularly identified as one of the ingredients or components of effective instruction.

What many teachers do not know is that students value the dimensions of caring more highly than teachers do. Teachers tend to focus on the instructional aspects of their role—they want their courses to have standards, to be well organized; they want their instruction to be clear and effective at stimulating student interest.

Students agree that these aspects of instruction are important, but they consider the personal aspects of teaching just as important. They want teachers who welcome their questions, who acknowledge their input, and who are available—in short, teachers who establish rapport with individual students and the class as a whole. Said succinctly, caring is more important to students than it is to professors, according to a variety of research findings reviewed in this article.

But should faculty be concerned about what students consider important? Research findings say yes. One study cited reported that when instructor-student rapport increases, those increases are associated with greater student enjoyment of the class, improved attendance and attention, more study time devoted to the class, and more courses taken in that discipline.

Another study documented that a professor's positive attitude toward students accounted for 58 percent of the variability in the students' motivation, 42 percent of the variability in course appreciation, and 60 percent of students' attitude about the instructor. (p. 206)

Meyers addresses three faculty criticisms and cautions about caring, starting with **"My students don't appreciate how much I care."** The problem here, according to Meyers, is that faculty don't always express their care in ways that students understand. Faculty express caring through their devotion to the instructional aspects of their role. They always come to class prepared. They devote time and energy to keeping current in their field. They spend countless hours reading and reviewing potential texts.

Those commitments bespeak their care, but according to the research, those are not the behaviors students associate with caring. Research on something called "verbal immediacy" has identified a number of behaviors that do convey caring to students—things such as using personal examples, asking questions and encouraging students to talk, using humor in class, addressing students by name, and many others listed in a table in the article—and Meyers recommends that faculty consider using more of these behaviors.

Some faculty members are reluctant to express care for students because they don't want to get too close to students. And Meyers agrees: "Faculty must maintain an awareness of interpersonal boundaries when creating supportive relationships with students." (p. 207) It's a question of finding an appropriate balance between caring for students and maintaining professional boundaries. Meyers offers this advice: "Effective, caring faculty members balance their connection with students by setting limits as needed, by enforcing classroom policies in consistent and equitable ways, and by maintaining democratic and respectful authority in the college classroom." (p. 207)

And finally, there are faculty who believe **"My job is to teach, not to care."** These faculty members worry that caring compromises academic rigor and lowers standards. They think that caring means always being nice, never pushing students, and always avoiding criticism.

But it's not a case of either-or—caring or doing those things associated with the instructional role. Teachers should do both because students benefit enormously when they do. And caring benefits teachers as well. Research has documented that when faculty don't care or fail to communicate their concern for students, students respond in kind. When students don't care about the teacher, they are much more willing to disrupt the class and make learning more difficult for everyone.

This is a first-rate article that convincingly establishes the importance of caring in the college classroom. It ends with an interesting set of questions on the topic that would make for excellent discussion with colleagues.

Reference: Meyers, S.A. (2009). "Do Your Students Care Whether You Care about Them?" **College Teaching,** 57 (4), 205–210.

Reprinted from *The Teaching Professor*, 25.5 (2011): 5.

Teaching Mindfulness in College Classrooms

By Robert Yoder and Jami Cotler, Siena College, New York; and Patti Vitale, Brown School, New York

Pressures and constant distractions are a significant part of the lives of American students of all ages. For college students, learning how to balance school, jobs, and relationships is stressful; social networks and cell phones constantly interrupt the current focus of attention. Academic performance suffers when feelings and distractions filter out lecture content and impede studying. Recent reports of increases in young adult depression, anxiety, attention deficit disorders, and social problems are compelling college teachers to explore methods for guiding students to better understand their minds and how they think.

Grounded in Buddhist teachings, the art of mindfulness is beginning to take root in Western culture. Mindfulness can be described as calm awareness of the present moment and cultivating positive feelings such as compassion and patience. Mindfulness techniques can reduce stress and focus attention on the current task. Since successful teaching requires an environment conducive to learning, it is useful to employ techniques to calm students, improve their capacity to resolve conflicts, and teach them more about how their minds function.

The Hawn Foundation (*www.hawnfoundation.org*) is spearheading an effort to create awareness of these benefits and is developing resources for elementary schools to implement mindful teaching techniques throughout their curricula and throughout the student's day. This program, called MindUP®, teaches children strategies for dealing with stress, disappointment, and conflict.

MindUP has four central goals: (1) foster mindful, focused awareness without judgment; (2) increase positive human qualities such as empathy, perspective taking, and kindness; (3) increase optimism and well-being; and

(4) foster a cohesive, caring classroom climate that enhances learning. We propose the application of certain MindUP techniques in the college classroom.

According to a recent survey of research (referenced at the end of the article) about the benefits of mindful meditation in higher education, mindful meditation has shown positive results as a way to handle academic stress, depression, and drug addiction and to regulate high blood pressure. One study documented improved GPAs with a group of college students who received meditation instruction and practice, compared with a control group.

We use the word "meditation" in a secular manner, as a way to calm the mind in "relaxed attention," increasing awareness and presence. Distracting thoughts are acknowledged but not given mental energy; they are allowed to pass without invoking new thoughts or associations. This training includes techniques that allow students to improve their own emotional health and ability to learn.

Here are some of the strategies we've used in our college-level classrooms to provide calm and attentive learning environments:

1) Breathing exercises and a bell or tone to introduce meditation or breathing.
   Invite students to sit quietly upright, eyes closed, remaining still and gently focusing on their breath, each inhale and exhale, for one to three minutes. Some students may feel self-conscious but will join in after some of their classmates do. Before exams, lead students in stretching and breathing exercises at their seats to increase their performance. You can use breathing strategies to manage the classroom when students interrupt teaching, struggle with assignments, or have conflicts with other students.

2) A "joy" or "gratitude" stone passed around class.
   The instructor starts and invites each student to hold the stone and say something he or she is grateful for, and then the student hands the stone to the next student. We hope that students will learn to be grateful for family and friends rather than for material objects. Eventually, we can extend this practice to serving the community at large, which is a tenet of the MindUP program and part of the mission of many colleges.

3) Creative visualization techniques and compassion generation.
   The instructor can include beautiful images and calming musical in-

terludes in lectures to delight students' minds and create alert attentiveness. Invite students to imagine being successful in school, relationships, and careers. Especially important to visual learners, imagery can be used to augment many different classroom lessons.

Despite the many documented benefits of a regimen of mindfulness, it is rarely taught in an academic setting. Self-reflection, compassion, and a long-term view may become critical skills for the future development of mankind. As Goldie Hawn so clearly points out, "We need to rethink our approach to classroom education by integrating neuroscience with the latest social and emotional learning techniques. A peaceful, happy child is the first step toward a peaceful world."

Reference: Shapiro, S., Brown, K., Astin, J. (2008). *Toward the Integration of Meditation into Higher Education: A Review of Research.* Retrieved from *www.contemplativemind.org/admin/wp-content/uploads/2012/09/ MedandHigherEd.pdf.*

Reprinted from *The Teaching Professor,* 25.3 (2011): 1.

Honoring and Challenging Students' Beliefs

By Natasha Flowers, Indiana University-Purdue University Indianapolis, Indiana

Students walk into college classrooms with values and beliefs that are non-negotiable. They do not see themselves as broken vessels, blank slates, or empty cups ready for filling. Many students whom I have encountered accept that they may not know everything, but they still seek affirmation that their experiences and beliefs are valid. In any course, there is room for students to doubt and dismiss ideas that contradict what they hold most dear. As educators, we must consider their starting points in order for our dialogues with them to be more authentic.

When they begin reading the content and discussing it in class, it is important to have some framework that describes how the course will honor and challenge their beliefs. This framework can also benefit the design of in-class activities and graded assignments.

Over time, I have begun explicitly emphasizing the need to balance and integrate these three components: (1) personal experiences, beliefs, and values; (2) others' experiences and values; and (3) the expertise of scholars and practitioners. Using a triangle as the visual, I propose that each component has its own point and is equally valuable. Throughout the semester, this framework anchors our discussions.

"You are not broken."

After semesters of hearing students use derogatory remarks or question the integrity of an entire group of people, it's tempting to consider them ignorant and lose respect for them. But if we communicate these impressions, students feel belittled or pressured to regurgitate what they think we want them to think.

These results are not productive if the goal is to deepen understanding and self-reflection. While students are learning new material, small- and whole-group activities can encourage thoughtful examination of the content through their own personal experiences and their own value systems.

"That person's shoes are hard to walk in."

As children, most of us learned about the misplaced curiosity of Goldilocks in her pursuit of a different experience. Her exploration of bear culture is actually a glimpse into how to disrespect what and whom we are trying to get to know.

However, when we ask students to walk in another person's shoes as part of developing their awareness of others, we must remember how uncomfortable that can be, especially if someone else's experience does not afford the comforts that our own lives offer (ergo, the piping-hot porridge and a rock-hard bed).

In class, having students make a T-chart that lists the ways in which they operate and how they would describe the exact opposite may help them see how they perceive others. For example, one of my students shared that she was highly motivated and highly organized and described the opposite person as detached and lazy. What a telling assignment! Last, having students read a memoir or semiautobiographical work that represents diverse cultural experiences will emphasize thoughtfulness and respect for commonalities and diversity within and across communities.

"Scholars and practitioners have values too."

Each semester, students buy books and download articles with the expectation that some expert will enlighten them. Nonetheless, any professional course can further honor and challenge students' beliefs and values with a reminder that scholars and practitioners are people too.

I assign articles and chapters that explore the positions the authors have taken, their identities, and their experiences as researchers and professionals in the field. These perspectives are key when asking students to believe the words of the experts. Students' knowledge of the experts' personal connections or roles as outsiders is just as important as the results of any study.

Balancing three sharp points

In order to emphasize the importance of balance, it is critical to have a frank conversation about what the imbalance may look like. If students are focused solely on their own perspectives, they risk having or nurturing an egocentric and ethnocentric perspective. How can their research and practice benefit anyone if they do not value others' ways of knowing or doing?

Second, the narrow focus on other people's perspectives may initially increase interest in diversity, but students must understand the danger of not seeing possible ways in which they may connect with others.

Last, it is possible for students to value the expertise of the scholars and practitioners at the expense of dismissing the real-life experiences of themselves and others. While in college, it is important to have students see how their journeys may contribute to their fields even before they have obtained their degrees.

This appears to be an easy formula, but the trick is in the careful monitoring of your own and your students' use of each major perspective in papers and discussions. This formula allows me to consider my own biases and values as well as my expectations of undergraduates in professional programs.

Reprinted from *The Teaching Professor*, 25.3 (2011): 6.

When Teachers Are 'Present'

By Maryellen Weimer, Penn State Berks, Pennsylvania

"Without presence, teachers are like guides in a theme park who tell the same joke a dozen times a day. We're there, but we're not there. With presence, teaching lives, it may or may not be good teaching, but it's alive." (p. 215) Jerry Farber makes this observation in the opening paragraphs of a "commentary" on teaching and presence.

Presence, as he defines it, is not poise or confidence but the sense of immediacy, openness, and spontaneity a teacher brings to the classroom. This kind of presence is elusive, easily eroded by repetition and sameness. And there's a great deal of repetition and sameness in teaching—the same pieces of literature, fundamental readings, problems, basic concepts, underlying questions, and foundational facts that teachers must get through course after course, semester after semester, year after year.

A carefully crafted set of questions can lead to a stimulating, provocative, and memorable discussion. But use those same questions four or five times and their intellectual edginess dulls. Most of the answers are no longer fresh. Farber describes what happens this way: "Questions and answers become merely instruments. We're not really asking and we're not really listening. We're like travelers keeping one eye on the map and another on the clock as the countryside blurs by outside the window." (p. 218)

These notions of presence collide with the idea of performance. Even skilled performers do not automatically have presence. Nor is presence presumed by certain techniques or excluded by others. It is not a case of using active learning and abandoning lecture.

"I've had more than enough opportunity to observe (and to hear countless reports of) 'active learning' sessions that are at least as alienating and unproductive as the droning, read-from-yellowing-notes lecture that is so often invoked as a foil by the people who give the teaching workshops. The problem, as always, is pedagogical mindlessness." (p. 231)

It's not that Farber is against active learning. His point is simply that teachers can be present or absent when using any approach, in any classroom or course. In that sense, presence is independent of method or content, and yet it can be born of either.

Farber's article is really about one of the most challenging (and ignored) aspects of teaching—how to keep it fresh and invigorated for the long haul. Not only is this kind of vibrancy essential for the teacher's well-being, but its presence or absence also makes a difference to students.

"When we're absent, when we're there but not there, this, in effect, excludes the students, who are reduced to the role of mere onlookers (in lecture) or objects to be manipulated (in 'class-centered' activities)." (p. 216)

Given its importance to teacher and student, is there any way to cultivate this sense of aliveness and vitality in the classroom? Farber suggests three things, none of which involves techniques per se.

First, in his experience, he has found presence is more likely if he is unwilling to settle for less. This means he holds "every single class session up to the standard of the best I've been able to achieve." (p. 219) He doesn't get depressed if the class doesn't reach that high standard, recognizing that realistically not every day will be the best, but he doesn't give himself permission to aim for something less.

Second, he recommends being as aware as possible of the people in the room and "how they, collectively and individually, seem to be engaging with what's going on." (p. 219) Lots of times we teach only to those students who are with us, the ones who are listening, nodding, asking questions, and taking notes. Presence in the classroom acknowledges how everyone is responding. "The classroom is a social space of dizzying complexity; as much as possible, we want to remain conscious of this." (p. 220)

And finally, Farber believes presence comes when he stays in touch with his own sources of energy for that day and moment. "Presence demands not only that we take account of those people in the classroom with us at this particular moment, but that we take account of this moment in our own life as well. Presence requires that we find our own energy if we hope for the others in the room to find theirs." (p. 220)

Being present makes us vulnerable, which means it's a risky endeavor. "So we wrap ourselves in whatever insulation comes to hand; a formal and forbidding, or even arrogant, manner; an inflexible agenda; a set of props, videos, PowerPoint presentations, whatever, workshop, or other small group activities."

In order to discover these protections that may keep us safe but also prevent presence, Farber suggests we ask of them "Do they energize the class, give it intensity and focus?" (p. 223)

Reference: Farber, J. (2008). "Teaching and presence." **Pedagogy**, 8 (2), 215–225.

Reprinted from *The Teaching Professor*, 22.8 (2008): 4.

Chapter 3: Managing Challenging Behavior

Could We Hear from Somebody Else, Please?

By Elayne Shapiro, University of Portland, Oregon

Generating participation in a large class discussion is fraught with teaching land mines. We can call on people who raise their hands, but too often it is always the same people. We can ask to hear from someone else and risk offending those who have been volunteering, so that there are even fewer hands. We can call on people randomly and risk embarrassing those who aren't prepared or don't understand. Maybe that will motivate them to prepare, or it may just be reflected in our teaching evaluations.

I'd like to share an exercise that broadens class participation and offers a way around these potential risks.

The exercise originated as the children's game where one person starts a story, stops wherever he wants, and the next person picks up the story line. In college classrooms the story students pass to one another might be an explanation of a historical event, a description of a physiological process, or the suggested solution to a case study. In my course, it revolved around conceptual elements in a theory. Let me explain how I used the exercise.

During the first half of the session, I lectured about the concept "face theory." Next, I divided the class into thirds and told them they were going to be watching one of three film clips. Each group was assigned a different film vignette. All the groups were to use what they saw on their film clip to discuss these three issues.

1. How do positive and negative face function for each character?
2. Using face-saving goals (save own face, save other's face, damage own face, damage other's face), describe what happened.
3. Identify examples of resisting intimidation, refusing to step back, or suppressing conflict for harmony's sake.

After the clip, one group member began by answering the first question. This first person could stop at any time. The next person in the row picked up where the first group member had left off. Again, that group member could say as little or as much as he or she wished about the application of the theory to the vignette. Each group member could modify or amplify what the person before him or her had said, or the new speaker could move on to another element of the theory.

Students seemed to gauge how much was left to be covered and how many students still had to speak, resulting in most of the students in the group contributing to the conversation. The atmosphere was light, and students were highly attentive, wondering when the cutoff would come and how the next person would pick up the thread.

In sum, the exercise provided an opportunity to review and apply conceptual material. It resulted in most of the class participating without my having to censure students who typically dominate or my pleading for other participants. Students did not find the activity threatening—they were in control of how much they said. I was so pleased with how the activity went that I promptly decided to share the details in this short piece.

Reprinted from *The Teaching Professor,* 21.0 (2007): 3.

Solutions for Student Incivility

By Christy Price, Dalton State College, Georgia

In my workshops and presentations to faculty on engaging Millennial learners, I have been surprised how frequently the topic turns to student incivility. It seems everyone can tell a story of flagrant student disrespect. I have trouble relating to these experiences. In any given semester, I have approximately 200 students, and the vast majority of them are extremely cooperative, conscientious, and excited about their learning. In my 18 years of teaching, I have experienced what I would describe as uncivil student behavior in class on only two occasions.

Maybe I've just been lucky, but perhaps not. What if there were a formula for preventing or at least minimizing student incivility? Well, pull out your highlighter, because in my research on Millennial learners, I think I may have stumbled upon some answers.

Step 1: Shift your paradigm to prevention.

The first tip: don't take these behaviors personally. One of my colleagues has suggested the word incivility implies a specific choice or intention on the part of the student. Perhaps it would behoove us to describe these behaviors as "unproductive to the learning environment," since students often cluelessly exhibit them without realizing how their behavior is perceived and impacts the learning environment.

In addition, many faculty are concerned with very specific student types such as the belligerent student, the Neanderthal who makes offensive comments, the know-it-all, the verbal dominator, the class-skipper, the perpetually late, the early leaver, the talker, the texter, the sleeper, the newspaper reader, the Web surfer, the unprepared, or the student who demands special treatment.

We may find ways to successfully respond to and alter each specific behavior, but if we really wish to create a learning environment, we need to focus on holistic measures as opposed to fragmented reactions to specific infractions.

Step 2: Practice verbal judo—producing closeness as opposed to distance.

Recently a colleague relayed a story in which she asked her students to define multicultural education. One student replied, *"It is a Marxist plot to undermine public education."* Many of us might be quick to attack this perspective; however, we need to practice what I call "verbal judo."

We need our body language, tone, and words to send a message that de-escalates conflict. The Millennial learners I interview regularly describe antagonistic professorial responses to what they perceive as accidental or minor infractions. There's a lesson to learn here: never be defensive, reactionary, or express a strongly negative emotional tone with a student.

I frequently hear professors describe with bravado interactions in which they criticize, humiliate, deride, and belittle the very people they are charged to teach, develop, and inspire. Every interaction we have with students produces either closeness or distance. The more we engage in distance-producing interactions with students, the more we can expect noncompliance and unproductive student behaviors in return.

We may win small battles, but we set ourselves up for losing the war as we lessen our overall ability to assist students in achieving the intended learning outcomes of our courses.

Step 3: Clearly communicate course policies and assignments with rationales, and consistently administer consequences.

An ounce of prevention will avert a ton of student angst if we provide rationales and consequences for assignments and policies. If we don't want students to challenge our grading procedures, a detailed rubric along with the reason for each assignment will clarify what students need to do and go a long way toward preventing student grade challenges after the fact. For example, if we have a policy that students lose points for late assignments, we should provide a policy rationale such as this on the course syllabus and assignment rubric: "In order to be fair to students who work to turn in assignments on time, late papers will lose 5 percent for each class day they are late."

Step 4: Design courses and utilize methods with the prevention of incivility in mind.

I have encountered professors who exhibit a wide range of attitudes and responses regarding specific behaviors such as texting in class. On one end of the spectrum are professors who don't care whether students text and successfully ignore such behaviors; on the other end are those who are disturbed beyond belief, who respond to texting with extremely punitive methods.

It has become painfully apparent to me that our methods play a powerful role in contributing to or averting unproductive student behaviors in the classroom. For example, I recently used my clicker response system to gather feedback from students regarding texting. Of the 77 students polled, 18 percent said they never text in their classes.

This was a shockingly low number from my perspective. As for the 63 texters, 87 percent strongly agreed or agreed with this statement: "I text more in classes in which the professor's main method is lecture and less in those classes where the professor uses a variety of methods such as discussion, group work, cases, and video or multimedia."

Conclusion

If you peruse the literature on college student incivility, you will find a great deal of evidence that supports these recommendations. Communicating clearly and providing a rationale for class policies, creating closeness as opposed to distance when interacting with students, and using engaging methods will not only lessen student incivility but also will help us achieve our ultimate goal of helping students learn while they are in college.

Reprinted from *The Teaching Professor*, 25.7 (2011): 6.

Entitled: Ways to Respond to Students Who Think They Are

Maryellen Weimer, Penn State Berks, Pennsylvania

Student entitlement can be defined academically: "a self-centered disposition characterized by a general disregard for traditional faculty relationship boundaries and authority" (p. 198), or it can be described more functionally: "a sense that they [students] deserve what they want because they want it and want it now." (p. 197)

Examples illustrate what many faculty have experienced with these students: complaints because a 2:00 a.m. email was not answered before an 8:00 a.m. class; wanting effort to count for points and credit ("But I tried, I really tried to find those references"); or requests to be exempted from requirements (such as course prerequisites) because "I don't need that course."

Students who arrive in college with this sense of entitlement are not a majority, and any consideration of how to respond to these students needs to be measured against how those responses will affect the learning environment for other students. The authors of a well-referenced article on student entitlement estimate that fewer than 10 percent of students fall into this category, but they point out that these students tend to require "a far greater proportion" of a faculty member's time and energy.

The article includes a useful discussion of the bases for this sense of entitlement. The authors see it as resulting from cultural norms and expectations, specifically the consumer mentality that characterizes how students orient to college. It's no longer about intellectual experiences; a college degree is now seen as a "ticket" to a better job.

Universities must now compete for students, and they do so by "selling" a college experience that comes with fancier living accommodations, extensive choices for food, 24-hour fitness centers, and so on. They also see grade inflation as contributing to students' senses of entitlement. Show up and do the work even at a minimal level and you can expect to get a B. And finally they discuss generational differences and document an increase in levels of narcissism among college students today.

The authors suggest six strategies for responding to students with a sense of entitlement. Each is briefly highlighted here, with many more details appearing in the article.

Make expectations explicit. The best place to begin doing this is on the syllabus. The authors recommend using grading rubrics that break assignments into parts and then designate a value for each component. Rubrics make expectations clear, but they also help instructors explain grading decisions to students. They can be used to structure those conversations.

Give students something to lose by negotiating. Entitled students often ask for grade changes or to have their work reevaluated. There is also some evidence that when students argue for more points with professors, they typically get some.

What the authors recommend is that faculty members agree to reevaluate work, but that reassessment may result in the grade being raised or the grade being lowered (or it may stay the same). Entitled students ask for reevaluations of their work because they have nothing to lose. This strategy introduces the possibility that there might be something lost, and this gives students pause before making the request.

Provide examples of "excellent" work. Many college students, especially beginning ones, do not have an accurate sense of the quality of their work. It may well be that they worked harder on this paper than on any other they've ever written, but it still may be well below college standards.

Examples can be used to show students the differences between what they have done and what happens in an A paper. If these "excellent" examples are provided after students have done the assignment, this prevents students from attempting to copy the format without developing their own frameworks.

Ask students to make the case first in writing. If students believe their works merits more points than have been awarded, don't have a discussion with them about that until they have explained why in writing. This helps defuse the emotion that often accompanies these exchanges, and it enables both the student and faculty member to prepare for the conversation.

Re-socialize students and faculty. "Explain your philosophy of teaching and learning and your focus on student responsibility. ... Socialize students into assuming responsibility for their own efforts and their own learning so that they are less likely to blame you for any shortcomings." (p. 202) That's re-socializing students—for faculty, the authors recommend attempting to understand today's college students better. That doesn't mean accepting behavior that compromises the educational enterprise, but it does mean coming to grips with who these students are.

Institutional responses. The authors believe that institutional climate plays a role in determining how students behave and that certain climates diminish the amount of entitlement students may feel. They use rigorous first-year seminars as an example of how some institutions establish intellectual expectations for students.

The authors conclude by reiterating that this sense of entitlement is not characteristic of all college students. When faculty consider strategies that respond to entitlement, they must do so with an eye toward the learning needs of those students who come to college expecting their courses to be work and their thinking to be challenged.

Reference: Lippmann, S., Bulanda, R.E., and Wagenaar, T.C. (2009). "Student entitlement: Issues and strategies for confronting entitlement in the classroom and beyond." *College Teaching*, 57 (4), 197–203.

Reprinted from *The Teaching Professor,* 25.7 (2011): 8.

Psychological Perspectives on Managing Classroom Conflict

By Jim Guinee, University of Central Arkansas, Arkansas

For the past 10 years I've given a presentation on managing classroom conflict to new faculty at my institution. I'm a psychologist, so that's the unique perspective I offer. Throughout the presentation I emphasize the need to analyze "cognitive errors," which I define as the faulty assumptions or misinterpretations commonly made by new (and not-so-new) faculty. These ways of responding to negative student behavior are ineffective; sometimes they even make it worse. I'd like to highlight several of these.

Most new faculty want to come across as being nice. When negative behaviors surface, they secretly hope they will disappear, particularly due to the mistaken belief that being nice and being respected always go hand in hand. Unfortunately, generally the negative behavior not only doesn't disappear, but it gets transmitted to other students like a virus.

Then there's the error I call the "misperception of colleague individuality." Each class, each teacher, has a different set of rules. For example, some instructors ban laptops from the classroom, while others require students with laptops to sit in the front row, and still others do not allow makeups under any circumstances. Then there are those teachers who don't specify any policies either verbally or in writing.

For students who encounter a different set of rules in every class, it's confusing. That's why I advise new (and experienced) instructors to be very explicit in the syllabus regarding classroom rules and consequences (e.g., cell phones, leaving class early).

Finally, new instructors tend to personalize negative behavior from students. For example, a student may be taking 15 hours and working full-time to pay the bills. Is it any surprise that this student dozes off during an afternoon class? How should an instructor interpret this behavior?

That's an important question, because how a teacher reacts depends on how he or she interprets the behavior. In this case I'd say you might want to give the student the benefit of the doubt. Don't immediately see this as a student problem. You may still need to wake up the student, but that's not because you put him or her to sleep.

I also offer new instructors a variety of helpful suggestions, many focused on the relationship that exists between teacher and student and the behavioral responses that are important in most interpersonal relationships. For example, I recommend specifically disclosing to another person your "issues" or "pet peeves." On the first day of class I share with students something I call "10 simple rules for taking my class."

One of the rules is *"Stay seated unless you see smoke."* No doubt every instructor has encountered students who for various reasons feel it necessary to begin packing up before class is dismissed. Early on in my teaching career I realized not only that I found it distracting, but it also made me ANGRY. Therefore I do what we call in counseling "owning" the problem. I acknowledge to the students that it is something that bothers ME, therefore it is MY problem. Amazingly this proves to be very effective and almost completely eliminates the behavior from ever occurring.

Although we've been discussing common behavior problems, students are not always in complete control of their behavior. Some negative student behavior is the result of psychological problems. My experience with new faculty is that they are often compassionate and want to help, but they are afraid they might offend the student.

They also feel a bit reluctant to discuss personal issues with students. On my campus, we have a link on our website specifically for assisting faculty with counseling center referrals [http://uca.edu/counseling/resources/how-to-make-a-referral/]. We encourage faculty to call and discuss observations, and we suggest strategies for responding to a troubled student.

In conclusion, I recommend improving classroom management by examining the individual you are in control of—yourself. By looking at such areas as distorted thinking, disclosure to students, and behavioral changes, you can effect much positive change in the classroom and do so without even getting involved with students over the behavior issues.

Reprinted from *The Teaching Professor*, 25.8 (2011): 1.

Dealing with Interested but Noncompliant Students

By Carl B. Bridges, Johnson Bible College, Tennessee

If you have been teaching for any time at all, I'll bet you've encountered what I call the interested but noncompliant student (hereafter, the INC). Here are some examples encountered in my courses: In an ancient language course, one INC would not take the trouble to learn her noun forms and verb endings but, fascinated by the language, went online to find an inscription that she tried to decipher.

Another INC read more than I have in a subdivision of my field. He wanted to talk about it endlessly before and after class, so much so that I had to chase him away to give other students a chance to talk to me. Still another INC turned every writing assignment into a paper on his pet subject, about which he had read dozens of books. Am I describing student behaviors that sound familiar?

Sometimes, INCs are the brightest students in the class, but they may have the poorest attendance records. They may not read what's been assigned because they've discovered something else in the field that interests them more and are busy reading that. They may shine in class discussion but have not mastered the specifics they need to know in order to understand the content.

The question is, how do you deal with INCs? Teachers can take an authoritarian approach and treat them like any other students who don't do the assigned work. I don't recommend this approach because it will likely kill their interest in the course. Maybe it's better to follow their interests and let them set their own agenda for the course.

I don't endorse this approach either, because every field has basic concepts that anyone interested in the field is expected to know. It seems to me we need to come at these INCs from two directions at once. Let me explain.

Student interest in a subject is a beautiful and fragile thing; it shouldn't be squandered. In some situations and with some areas of study, we can allow an INC to customize the assignments, so long as that student has already covered the basics in his or her own reading. Based on my experiences, I'd like to offer some suggestions and advice:

- Assign the INC a nonstandard research project and have him or her present it to the class.
- Allow the INC to substitute one reading for another.
- Ask the INC to tutor students who may be struggling with course material that the INC has mastered.
- Give the INC an opportunity to facilitate or share more at length in classroom discussions when he or she knows a lot about the topic.
- Above all, treat the INC with respect as a fellow learner.

At the same time, INCs must be held to standards determined by the teacher. We are the content experts and know what knowledge students need to take from our courses if they are to do well in subsequent courses or the field in general. In addition, we open ourselves up to charges of favoritism when we allow one student to do what he or she wishes or appear to give that student instructor-like status.

If the course has an attendance policy, it needs to apply equally to everyone. All tests are graded the same way. It may be wise to let alternative assignments and readings negotiated with the INCs be a private matter between those students and the teacher.

We must not forget that it is still possible for a bright, interested student to fail a course. That student may not be willing to meet the goals and objectives of the course, even if that student and the instructor have agreed upon alternative ways of meeting those goals and objectives. Instructors do not give grades, passing or otherwise. Students earn them.

Interested but noncompliant students: Are they a source of annoyance or an instructional opportunity? Both, I think, but with a little forethought we can minimize the annoyance and maximize the opportunity.

Reprinted from The *Teaching Professor,* 23.1 (2009): 2.

A Behavior Contract that Made a Difference

By Lori Norin and Tom Walton, University of Arkansas-Fort Smith, Arkansas

It seemed that almost every day we would come back to our offices after our speech classes with a frown on our faces and the need to tell a story about the latest shenanigans that happened in class. A student "accidentally" showed an inappropriate image on a PowerPoint slide during his speech. A student walked in 20 minutes late during a classmate's speech—with a pizza in one hand, a Mountain Dew in the other, and a cell phone on one ear. A student refused to give her speech as scheduled and dared us to do something about it.

Finally, one day we decided we had had enough. We created a list of behavioral expectations, which we asked students to sign, and thus was born the Speech Department Behavior Contract. Since then it has grown into a well-defined instrument that has had as much impact on student retention, success, and well-being as any other strategy we have added to the curriculum.

Initially the document contained 10 items—rudimentary things such as students taking responsibility for reading the syllabus, signing the attendance sheet, taking the pretests and pre-assessments, meeting deadlines, and understanding the consequences of making excuses for missing speeches.

Even in its early format, the contract positively impacted retention and behavior in the classroom as observed by us and noted by our dean. Students told us that they appreciated the precise listing of their responsibilities because it made the rules and consequences clear.

At the end of each semester, we revise the document based on the events of the previous semester. For example, we added a statement concerning the campus electronic policy based on a serious plagiarism case that occurred in one of our sections.

Once it became prevalent and blatant, we added a statement about text messaging in class. Some of our other colleagues are using contracts similar to ours, and they report the same positive effect. We hope that our sharing our contract will lead you to consider how it might help in creating an ideal learning environment in your classroom.

Speech Department Classroom Behavior Contract

1. I have received, read, and understand the general syllabus for the course, including the attendance policy.
2. I understand that failure to sign the attendance sheet at the appropriate time and date will result in my being marked absent.
3. I verify that my professor has requested that I meet with him or her first should I have any concerns about the conduct of the course. If that meeting does not resolve the concerns, then my professor will recommend I meet with the department's lead faculty member or department chair.
4. I understand that my professor expects respect for everyone in the classroom at all times. This includes rules about sleeping, inappropriate talking, rudeness, doing homework, answering cell phones, any disruptive behavior, and the like.
5. I understand it is my responsibility to take the online content pre- and post-test(s) by the assigned date(s).
6. I understand that it is my responsibility to complete the written pre- and post-assessment(s) (PRCA, speech anxiety, listening inventory) by the assigned date.
7. I understand that it is my responsibility to complete all assignments on time and that there are penalties for late assignments (if allowed) at each professor's discretion.
8. I agree that if I don't understand an assignment it is my responsibility to ask for clarification.
9. I understand my professor's policy about being tardy and the consequences of not following his or her policy.
10. I understand the ramifications of missing a scheduled speaking day.
11. I understand that should I miss class it is my responsibility to get any handouts or other materials.
12. I understand that it is my responsibility to check my email daily or weekly, depending on my professor's guidelines.
13. I understand that it is my responsibility to follow directions and that failure to do so will result in a loss of points.

14. I understand that it is my responsibility to read and follow the Electronic Communications Policy.
15. I understand that I should not enter the classroom during a student speech. I should wait to hear applause and then enter.
16. I understand that plagiarism of any kind will not be tolerated and may result in receiving a zero (0) for the assignment, withdrawal from the course, or suspension from the university.
17. I understand that cell phones must be turned off or turned to vibrate during class and that each professor may at his or her discretion enforce a consequence for any cell phone ringing or for text messaging during class.
18. I have read, understand, and agree to abide by the student handbook guidelines for classroom ethics.
19. I understand that each professor may add additional rules in writing to this departmental document.

Student Signature _____

Ed.'s note: The authors have graciously given individual faculty permission to use or revise their behavior contract. Permission to reprint or publish the contract must be requested from the copyright holder, Magna Publications, Inc.

Reprinted from *The Teaching Professor,* 21.8 (2007): 6.

Three Things to Do with Cell Phones (Besides Confiscate Them)

By Karen Eifler, University of Portland, Oregon

My class had just finished covering three chalkboards with a rather dazzling array of concept clusters, illustrations, and links among disparate ideas. Clearly, a lot of learning had been generated. As I picked up the eraser to clear the board, I mentioned it was too bad that Chelsea and Eric (who were absent) had missed this vibrant discussion.

"Well, if you promise not to bust me, Dr. E., I could take a picture of all this and send it to them," offered Claire. She pointed at the laminated sign in the front of the room that said in a huge font, complete with helpful picture, NO CELL PHONES ALLOWED IN CLASS.

Now, I am just as annoyed as the next person by the rude, thoughtless use of cell phones in public and have no patience with the thought of students using them to talk or text during my class.

But Claire's comment reminded me that most cell phones today are powerful little handheld computers, and, like any tool, I could put them to use to facilitate and enhance several aspects of the teaching and learning I want to happen in my classroom. That was a new insight for me. It motivated me to start using cell phones in class rather than just being offended by them. Let me share three simple ways they've helped my students and me in recent months:

1) **Archive content from the chalkboard or whiteboard by taking a picture of it, as in the vignette referenced above.** Sure, interactive Smart Boards offer the same option, but for those of us who do not teach in rooms equipped with those, the cell phone camera is a fine low-tech option. Sometimes classes yield tremendous spontaneous insights that we may want to draw upon later.

Claire sent the pictures to her classmates who missed class, and although I do not advocate making it easier on students who are absent, neither do I want them to miss out on crucial content. Claire also sent me the picture, and I have drawn upon this use of the cell phone frequently ever since, as now I have an artifact of teaching and learning and very often an image to use as a springboard into a new class session.

We have also used the cell phone cameras to capture 3-D structures and role plays that have come up in class to which we know we will want to refer later without necessarily saving the original items. The real coup was using my own cell phone camera to document the board notes from a freewheeling faculty meeting that would have otherwise vanished. My most anti-technology colleagues were pleasantly taken aback.

2) **Time small-group activities using the built-in clock functions.** In any group of three or four students, at least one (if not all) will have a cell phone. When we break out for intimate discussions or application tasks, I have the phone holders synchronize times and timers and then let the groups do their work.

This frees them from having to keep glancing at the room clock and keeps them more focused on the task. I have also experimented with all students using timers set on "vibrate" to monitor timed reading and individual in-class exercises and am pleased with the sense of calm this elicits, quite different from the tenser "countdown" atmosphere we have when I am the sole timekeeper.

3) **Google it.** There are times when what's happening in class veers in an unanticipated direction and we need a fact I simply do not have at my disposal, nor does anyone in class. If it's true that "all of us are smarter than one of us," then literally bringing in the world via the Internet capacities of my students' cell phones makes us collectively brilliant.

We can do a quick search to find the missing details and then move on. For readers concerned that the students might keep cyber-wandering once the fact is retrieved, I can report that having several students on the same hunt moves the process along, and once we have our answer, a swift application of the patented, expectant "teacher look" usually brings them back in.

It has also been instructive to probe and push and ponder when diligent students come up with differing facts. These are great teachable moments that help me underscore why their research must not begin and end with Wikipedia—and the evidence is right there in their hands.

The list above is hardly exhaustive, but perhaps it can help us begin to refocus the cell-phones-in-class conversation. New technologies require us to harness our wisdom and imagination. They also challenge us to think differently about what we do and why.

Based on what's happened in my classroom, I now propose that there are pedagogically defensible alternatives to silencing cell phones in our classrooms.

Reprinted from *The Teaching Professor,* 23.7 (2009): 3.

Police Officer or Professor?

By Peter J. Kakela, Michigan State University, Michigan

I'm not sure how to say this without appearing either arrogant or ignorant, but I have discovered that there is a difference between being a police officer and being a professor. I have recognized the difference for some time now, but it has taken me the better part of my 40 years as a college professor to feel fairly comfortable in my new skin.

For many years, I taught more like a police officer than a professor. I didn't want anyone in my classes to get higher grades than they deserved. I was a vigilant protector of academic integrity. I looked for students who did not come to class or who might be breaking the rules. I set traps with quizzes and tricky test questions.

Many of the multiple-choice questions I wrote focused on detailed, technical knowledge of facts. I paid little attention to the relevance of those facts. To pass these tests students needed to know exact terminology and specific definitions.

For example, when I taught Introduction to Physical Geography, I held students accountable for the facts despite all the wonderful material on weather and natural disasters; on plate tectonics and earth processes; on greenhouse gases, environmental pollution, and global warming. Encouraged by senior faculty, I wrote exam questions that tested students' ability to distinguish longitude from latitude, find locations, and deal with time zones.

Furthermore, I focused on the problem students—trying to catch the ones who were not learning or those who looked as though they might sneak through. Nobody was going to steal a grade in my courses. I was the police officer, and I made my students the criminals.

Taking this approach to education did not make me unique. A couple of years ago I was talking with a new faculty member in our department. Almost immediately she announced disdainfully, "I understand you can't get undergrads to read here." She was accusing students she had not even met of being slackers. At a luncheon ceremony a year ago, a group of my colleagues started talking about teaching.

One youngish faculty member began complaining that half his students didn't come to class. So he started putting his lecture notes online. However, he didn't put all the material online, so on his tests he could catch the ones who were reading only the Internet notes.

I could continue this list of examples, but at this point in my career I find them frustrating. I have stopped being so concerned with the problem students and now focus on the majority who are working hard and want to learn. Why should I devote most of my time and much of my energy to the few students who don't want to learn?

Keeping my attention focused on the slackers made me more tense and angry about my teaching. I was often discouraged, and my classrooms were not friendly places. Being a police officer did not make me happy.

Now I walk into class as a professor. I believe that the students in my class are there to learn. They want to know more about life and the world around them, about the environment, jobs, and careers they can enjoy for years to come. And I believe if we make learning fun, it brings out their creativity.

A relaxed mind can think better. Seeing their creativity inspires me—it makes me a better professor. Now I devote my energy to the students who are getting it, those who are bright, cheerful, relaxed, and interested in learning more. The shift has made teaching so much more enjoyable. And I'm convinced that more learning goes on in classrooms taught by professors, not by police officers.

Reprinted from *The Teaching Professor*, 22.2 (2008): 3.

Successful Classroom Management

By Jason Ebbeling, Menlo College, California, and Brian Van Brunt, Western Kentucky University, Kentucky

Managing students who are disruptive, those who lack motivation and appear as though they would rather be any place other than in the classroom, is easier when faculty take the right stance. Anything is possible when faculty have faith in the students they teach. Learning starts with a dedicated teacher interested in meeting the challenge of how to present content in a way that successfully navigates the barriers students erect.

Believing in students is the right stance, but it doesn't prevent students from coming to class unprepared, handing in assignments late, asking for exceptions, and talking in class. The principles of Motivational Enhancement Therapy, originally developed by W.R. Miller and S. Rollnick to help college professionals engage students with drinking problems, offer strategies that faculty can use with disruptive students in class.

Each of the four principles described below has the professor acknowledging the problem and then working with the student to develop a plan to correct the problem. It's an approach built on collaboration.

Express empathy—The professor communicates with the students from a position of power, but the professor still respects the student and practices active listening. Despite the power associated with being the professor, the teacher recognizes that the behavior that needs to be changed can be changed only by the student.

Develop discrepancy—Students are motivated to change when they perceive a discrepancy between where they are and where they want to be. The professor can make students aware of this discrepancy. "You want an A in this course, and yet you are regularly losing points by not being in class to take the quizzes." "You want to be a successful manager, and yet you fall asleep whenever you lose interest. What's going to happen when the staff meetings you're required to attend get boring?"

Avoid argumentation—Arguing with students only makes them more resistant. It is highly unlikely that the professor is going to persuade a student (whether that student needs to come to class or get work done on time). A more indirect approach may be better. "When you miss class, you are wasting money. You pay for each class and get nothing when you aren't there."

Roll with resistance—Don't meet it head on. Invite the student to think about the problem differently. Rather than imposing a solution, see whether the student might be able to generate one. "You missed the assignment. What's a fair consequence for that?"

College professors aren't law enforcement officers. They aren't expected to be entertainers or hand-holders. They do have the responsibility to create a classroom setting that engages students and fosters relationships based on mutual respect.

Students should not text in class or arrive late or hungover any more than professors should show up the minute class begins, lecture, and leave promptly when it's over. Learning occurs when both work together, treading softly on differences and celebrating strengths.

Reprinted from *The Teaching Professor*, 22.8 (2008): 4.

Chapter 4:
Strategies for
Student Engagement

Student Engagement: Trade-offs and Payoffs

By E. Shelley Reid, George Mason University, Virginia

I dread the moments when I look out into a classroom and see a collection of blank stares or thumbs clicking on tiny keypads: a pool of disengaged students, despite what I thought was a student-centered activity.

Recently, I have been considering how teachers (me specifically) undermine our own efforts to engage students. We do that by putting certain educational goals above getting and keeping students involved. If I sense a lack of energy and involvement on the part of students, right then I may need to adjust my teaching methods, even if that means sacrificing some other laudable goals.

Here are some examples that illustrate what I mean.

Engagement versus correctness

It's true enough that students need to be able to produce correct answers. They should know Thomas Jefferson's beliefs about representational government or how to set up a chemical equation. And asking questions is a great way to engage students, particularly the one who's answering the question. But some students may be too shy, unprepared, or indifferent to engage with a fact-based question. Plus, once it's answered, no more students need to engage.

We can, however, consciously craft engagement-focused questions rather than knowledge questions. These are *true questions* to which we don't know the answer; they have multiple "right" answers, and they relate to students' experiences.

They may also reveal comprehension or invite critical thinking: *What do you think is important for a democracy to survive? Which variable did you consider first in setting up this equation?* If necessary, I can give students 30 seconds to jot down an answer or share with a peer before I solicit responses.

Even when I accept all initial answers unreservedly—if I have designed the question well, the answers are all "right" for the students who gave them—I need not abandon correctness. I can then move us into critiquing the field, winnowing toward a "better" answer or a more "academic" response. This process is exactly what I am trying to teach students to do: not to take my word for it but to draw from their own experiences and reason toward a best answer.

Engagement versus coverage

The need for coverage presents another challenge: we have one class period to cover the Korean War or advanced research strategies, and we don't want to spend the whole period lecturing. Instead, I sometimes find myself pelting wary students with "Socratic" questions. In these situations, it may be both faster and more effective to do a shorter, non-interactive lecture and set aside five minutes for a related activity.

And when I engage students *before* I present information, I don't lose much speed. I start by asking student groups to pool what they already know about a problem: *List three tips for locating scholarly sources.*

Waiting for students to generate material takes time; I also worry about "the blind leading the blind." Yet students' collective knowledge can be surprisingly extensive. After hearing from students, I know better what I don't need to "cover" and can focus more efficiently on their questions or confusions.

Engagement versus consistency

We often ask student groups to report to the class, in part to ensure consistency in the learning experience. Wrong answers can be publicly set aside and core concepts reinforced. Yet sometimes those group reports act on engaged students like ice water on a newly lit fire. Likewise, our task lists for collaborative groups ensure consistent coverage, but speedy groups may still skimp on engagement so that they can sit back and engage with something other than content.

I can set aside consistency in favor of engagement: if my goal is that all students will engage in something for 10 minutes, then I may not need reports. Similarly, I may be able to provide students with more tasks or a larger problem than they can address in the allotted time and not worry about who has completed what steps.

When we move on, I can review questions or collect responses, but I don't need to. I've met my goal of engaging students in the material and can carry that momentum into the next segment of the class.

Engagement versus control

Making engagement the top priority means ceding some control over students' learning. Despite our ample qualifications to direct the learning endeavor, we also know that during the moments when we are most engaged in learning, we are often least engaged with our formal teachers or with anyone else's plans.

True free writes ("Write about anything"), group work with loose guidelines ("Talk about what surprised you in last night's reading"), and somewhat random engagement questions ("If you were going to paint a portrait, who would you paint?") may not push students to use concrete language, wrestle with critical concepts, or understand 18th-century European artwork.

That makes this the hardest trade for me to make. I need to remind myself that undirected engagement can be highly productive for learners. If I want my students to surprise me and to enjoy making unexpected discoveries—the hallmarks of engaged, lifelong learning—I need to take these chances and trust that the payoffs will be worth the risks.

Getting engaged

When the blahs strike, I try to look for a way to completely—albeit temporarily—abandon correctness, coverage, consistency, or control in favor of getting students engaged. Besides all the good learning that results, I feel a pedagogical rush when my students turn on their brains and produce new knowledge. We all get engaged, and we all move a bit closer to learning "happily ever after."

Participation: Revisiting the basics

Student participation in college courses is an instructor expectation in most classes. That doesn't always mean lots of students contribute or that what they say takes class discussions to new heights, but as a strategy that seeks to engage students, the use of participation is widespread.

Moreover, recent years have seen a rise in more detailed and explicit criteria being proposed for the assessment of participation. Discussions of the pros and cons of "cold calling" (soliciting participation from a student who has not volunteered to answer) have appeared in the literature, as have a variety of proposed strategies and techniques for ways to increase the number and quality of student contributions.

In a thoughtful article, Raymond Jones challenges teachers to revisit what they hope to accomplish with participation and then assess whether the way participation is being used accomplishes those goals. He suggests faculty use participation to advance four goals. First, there's **accountability.** "If we fear that students are not doing the assigned reading and that they are therefore 'unprepared' for class, we might impose a class participation requirement to hold them accountable." (p. 59) However, he doesn't think it's always clear to students what they should be prepared to do in class after having done the reading. He asks the question this way: "Does the assigned reading enable or empower them to accomplish something meaningful in class?" (p. 60)

Sometimes professors use participation as a means to **involve more students**. They want to solicit contributions from more than the four or five (or two or three) who regularly participate. One way to accomplish that goal involves asking more questions. Of course, simple, straightforward questions take less time.

But if the questions are not necessarily very thought-provoking, then student answers mirror the questions. If a simple understanding suffices, then students can be less diligent about their reading or homework. "It behooves us to consider whether there is a trade-off between getting more students talking and the importance of what we have them talking about." (p. 60)

Another intent of participation is to help students **recall information.** An example might be participation that occurs at the beginning of the period, when teachers try to make connections between the topic for today and content covered previously. Jones doesn't think these question-and-answer exchanges get most students focused on content. How many students actually speak? "In practice this type of discussion involves one student with one idea at a time. What are the majority of students doing and thinking about?"

Finally, some professors use participation intending that students will **grapple with ideas.** In this case the professor poses a challenging or provocative question and invites students to weigh in on the topic. On good days an exciting exchange may be the result. Students start connecting ideas, arguing with passion, or moving to consider other viewpoints. "But which students actually participated in this heady exchange? What evidence do you have about what most students were doing, or how most students were thinking, during this otherwise delightful give-and-take?" (p. 60)

Jones proceeds to revisit a variety of different types of participation, raising the same sort of challenging issues. It's not that he's against participation. He simply wants teachers to analyze whether participation goals are actually being accomplished in practice—to look for what might be contradictions between intentions, means, and results.

"We might say we want greater involvement with students, but if it is serial and singular in nature rather than concurrent and integrated, we are limiting rather than expanding involvement and reasoning." (p. 61)

Reference: Jones, R.C. (2008). "The 'why' of class participation: A question worth asking." *College Teaching*, 56 (1), 59–62.

Reprinted from *The Teaching Professor*, 22.2 (2008): 4.

TEACHING STRATEGIES FOR THE COLLEGE CLASSROOM |

Traffic Lights and Participation

By Maryellen Weimer, Penn State Berks, Pennsylvania

Virtually all of us who work to promote interaction and dialogue in the classroom are interested in strategies that help us facilitate these exchanges. Here's an intriguing set.

Reginald Litz, who teaches business administration courses, positions participation within a set of related activities. First, students read a case study (the focus of discussion in class) and several supplementary readings. Before class, they write a one-page essay in which they answer one of three study questions about the readings. These essays must be submitted at least 90 minutes before class begins.

During those 90 minutes, Litz reviews those essays, looking for insightful and provocative comments that he then uses to start and stimulate discussion in class. Unless the author writes "do not quote," Litz is free to use material from these essays. He acknowledges the author by name unless the student requests on the essay that his or her name not be mentioned.

Before the discussion starts in class, Litz has students convene in groups to share their initial reactions to the case. This helps students "warm up" for the whole class discussion. Litz uses a unique system to let students control how they participate in the class discussion. At the beginning of the course, he gives each student three name cards: one red, one yellow, and one green. Students write their names on all three.

In any given class session, students select one of the three colors. If they put up the red card, that indicates that they do not wish to be called on. A yellow card means they are willing to contribute, but they do not welcome in-depth interrogation by the instructor. Green cards invite "unrestricted in-depth interrogation by the instructor." (p. 368)

There are grade implications that accompany each color choice: two points for green cards, one point for yellow, and no points for red. Class begins with Litz quoting from one of the student essays and asking the author to elaborate further on that quote. Others are then invited to join the discussion.

Finally, in this system students prepare a single-page, post-class essay in which they reflect on the class discussion. These essays encourage students (even those not actively participating) to listen to the discussion of the case. Like the other essays, these are due 90 minutes before the next class session, and Litz may read well-written ones at the beginning of the next class.

The obvious liability with a system such as this is the work involved in reviewing and grading all the essays. Litz makes this manageable in two ways. First, he uses a pass/fail system on the essays. If the effort is superficial, the student fails.

Second, students complete no more than one pre- or post-class essay per week. Keeping track of who is responding with what color card also makes more work. Litz expedites this process by soliciting a student volunteer who records the color selected and number of contributions on a seating chart. He also involves students in a determination of the extent of their participation at the end of the course.

For Litz, the goal of these techniques is to "create as positive a learning experience as possible. To that end, I seek to encourage students to reflect upon the material studied and then contribute to the class discussion when they feel ready." (p. 372)

Reference: Litz, R.A. (2003). "Red light, green light and other ideas for class participation–intensive courses: Method and implications for business ethics education." *Teaching Business Ethics, 7* (4), 365–378.

Reprinted from *The Teaching Professor,* 22.7 (2208): 7.

Benefits of Using Classroom Assistants

By Ken MacMillan, University of Calgary, Alberta, Canada

I work in a department that regularly enrolls 250 students in first-year classes, as do many other departments in colleges and universities. In my case, the situation is complicated by a small graduate program, too few teaching assistants, and an inability to break the larger classes into smaller sections for discussion.

This makes for a very challenging teaching situation. I use groups in the large class one day per week. Since then, I have worked on solving the staff problem with senior undergraduate students. I call them classroom assistants (CAs).

The CAs are drawn from a competitive pool of applicants at the beginning of the term. They must be top academic students, seniors, and interested in helping first-year students develop an understanding of our discipline. They go through a competitive application and interview process. Usually I have around 15 applicants for two positions. After selection, the new CAs sign a contract that contains a list of roles and responsibilities. I expect CAs to respect the objectives of the course and positively reflect on the faculty, department, and institution when dealing with students.

The CAs work 50 hours over a 13-week term and are paid $10 per hour, roughly one-third of what their TA counterparts are making. They are provided with all the reading materials for the course and attend class on the days when I have students working in groups. I let them know in advance what tasks the students will face on those days.

Along with the TAs and me, they circulate among the students, keeping them focused, helping them with their work, and asking and answering questions about the course materials. They are invited to participate in the plenary discussion during the final 15 minutes of class. Much of their work is completed behind the scenes. They assess and record the results of the group work and random reading quizzes.

My use of CAs significantly improves the instructor-student ratio, which is especially important on days when students work in groups. Students in the class accept the presence of the CAs without question. To first-year students, seniors look quite advanced, and they give beginning students a glimmer of hope about the kind of students they may one day become.

The CAs have also taken a number of relevant courses in the department, and their appraisal of these courses sometimes seems more honest to students. In contrast, the instructor and TAs are removed from the students by age, education, and vocation, making it more difficult for them to relate to student concerns.

The CAs free up valuable hours of senior course staff time; while the instructor and TAs remain responsible for delivering lectures and doing the bulk of the grading for the course, the administrative work of the CAs makes it considerably easier to accomplish these tasks. CAs also provide useful feedback to me about how well the material is getting through, which has encouraged me to change the pace, order, and content of the lectures. I appreciate getting the feedback during the course as opposed to getting ratings results after the course has concluded.

There have been some challenges. Because nobody else in my department uses CAs, securing funding, modest as it is, is an annual hat-in-hand ritual that depends entirely on the current budget and the department head's support.

When I began this program a few years ago, there was excited talk of developing a senior seminar on university teaching in which students in their final year would work as CAs; read literature on pedagogy; discuss what they learned with one another in weekly meetings; and receive course credit based on written work, participation, and feedback from the instructors with whom they worked.

This had the advantage of making the CAs far more cost-effective while also giving the program some official sanction and pedagogical merit. Within a few months, the idea fizzled, as so many ideas do.

Some colleagues see the program as pragmatic and innovative, while others have expressed concern that it might reduce the quality of education in the department. Having seen the benefits of using CAs firsthand, I am convinced that the program has the potential to ease strained teaching and financial resources, provide senior students with valuable and relevant experience, and offer beginning students a key link to the senior course staff.

Reprinted from *The Teaching Professor,* 23.2 (2009): 6.

Daily Experts: Technique to Encourage Student Participation

By Angie Thompson, St. Francis Xavier University, Nova Scotia, Canada

If you're interested in approaches that encourage students to speak in class and develop their public-speaking skills, as well as techniques that help you learn student names, then my "daily experts" strategy may be of use to you.

What are daily experts? I list five or six students' names on a Power-Point slide at the beginning of my classes (which are large, 65 to 150 students). These individuals, assuming that they are in class, then become my daily experts—the first ones I ask questions or opinions of before opening discussion to the whole class. The approach provides for one-on-one dialogue in the midst of a larger class, creating an environment that encourages interaction.

In my first-year class, I tend to pose questions that review materials covered in the previous lecture. These questions are listed on PowerPoint, and I ask them at the beginning of class to remind everyone of the content we worked on in the previous class session. I often build on the students' responses, asking related questions and/or adding depth to the material myself. In my fourth-year classes, I may use daily experts to review as well.

More frequently, though, I ask them questions or inquire about their opinions in the middle or latter half of class after new content has been covered. These queries tend to be more application-oriented, often requiring lengthier responses from which I can build a class or small-group discussion.

Why use daily experts? For my first-year class, the main reason is to break the ice, which I hope helps students realize that I am approachable. It also ensures that each student has at least one opportunity to speak in front of the class. In my fourth-year classes, I use the daily experts concept to provide the same speaking experience, but more as a tool to ensure that all students have the chance to share relevant experiences and opinions with me and the rest of the class.

How does the professor benefit from daily experts? I get to know my students' names, and I am more likely to remember them outside class as well. Indirectly, my use of daily experts encourages class attendance. Students want to be there when their name appears on the PowerPoint. They don't want to hear from their classmates "You missed being a daily expert today" or to hear me say later, "I missed you in class yesterday…. you were one of my daily experts."

I also benefit because using daily experts forces me to teach in another way—a way that gets me focused on individuals. Every interaction with a daily expert becomes a teaching opportunity. It may be a chance to help that student become a bit more confident when he or she interacts with a professor. It's a chance to help students face and conquer that fear of speaking in class. Most important, the strategy gets students actively engaged with the class and its course materials.

What about the rest of the class? There are benefits to the whole class when I interact with my daily experts. It gives others the opportunity to learn classmates' names. They also benefit when they consider how they might have responded differently. They can learn from others' experiences and see how to ask questions in a nonthreatening way. The technique helps everyone engage more actively in the course material. So if you want your classes (even large ones) to be interactive, a daily expert approach might be just what you're looking for.

Reprinted from *The Teaching Professor*, 22.10 (2008): 2.

Truly Participatory Seminars

By Sarah M. Leupen and Edward H. Burtt, Jr., Ohio Wesleyan University, Ohio

In typical upper-division seminars, each week one student leads 10 to15 classmates in a discussion of an important research paper in the field or presents his or her own work to the group. Students not presenting are supposed to participate in the discussion but rarely do, despite professorial queries aimed at generating a lively, provocative exchange. Seminars using this format can be deadly dull. We decided to tackle the problem and would like to share our ideas for more interactive, exciting, and educationally enriching exchanges in seminars.

The most important change we made was to have every student present every week in one of three formats: one minute (approximately seven students per week), five minutes (three to four students per week), or 15 minutes (two students per week). In one minute, students present an idea or introduce an organism (we teach biology) that illustrates the topic of the week.

Time for questions following the one-minute presentation is unlimited. In five minutes, students are expected to present a more detailed, literature-based perspective on the topic, again with unlimited time for questions.

The 15-minute category is closest to the "traditional" paper presentation on a designated topic. One week before presentation, each presenter must provide a copy of the paper or post it on the seminar website for the rest of the class and faculty. After the paper is available, every student in the seminar must post one or more open-ended questions about the paper on the seminar website at least 48 hours before the class meets.

The student presenter is expected to address these questions in the presentation. After the 15-minute presentation, there is unlimited time for questions raised in the seminar. Inevitably, and delightfully, we find that the whole is greater than the sum of its parts. Without any puppet-string pulling by us, biological themes emerge from each seminar meeting. These flesh out the week's topic and unite the individual presentations.

We enforce time limits stringently, using a bell to warn students when they approach the limit. When the time is up, one of us begins to ring the bell furiously, thereby drowning out all conversation. As soon as the student stops, we proceed to questions. We make the bell ringing something of a show, thereby adding enough levity to relax the atmosphere and provide a bit of amusement. Nonetheless, the bell does effectively end the presentation.

The format ensures that all students come prepared and that all participate in the presentations and join in the discussions that follow. We use the number of questions each student asks during the seminar as an additional measure of participation and remind students that the quality of their questions is also a factor.

Finally, instead of writing a paper read only by the instructor, each student prepares a poster for presentation at a general session on the last evening of the seminar. During the first hour of the seminar, half the students stand with their posters while the instructors and half the students wander about listening to each presentation and asking questions. During the second hour, the students switch roles and we repeat the process.

Throughout the semester we emphasize participation by having students post preliminary questions to a seminar website, by having students present something at every meeting of the seminar, and by having all students prepare a poster for public display and open discussion. The result is a lively seminar in which most students ask questions, pose ideas, and actively discuss controversial issues.

The effect of having every student *present* every week is that every student is truly present every week—interested and engaged, with a "stake" in the proceedings. We and our students learn a great deal in these seminars and find that far from dozing through another long and boring paper, our evenings are filled with the excitement of exploring new material, debating important ideas, and finishing ahead of the bell!

Reprinted from *The Teaching Professor*, 22.8 (2008): 6.

Cell Phones in Class: Student Survey

By Maryellen Weimer, Penn State Berks, Pennsylvania

Cell phones in the classroom—it's a topic that generates much consternation among faculty. Are policies that prohibit their use enforceable? Are students texting in class? If so, how many? If a student is texting, does that distract other students? Are students using their phones to cheat? Are there any ways cell phones can be used to promote learning? The questions are many and the answers still a long way from definitive.

Most faculty have opinions about how much cell phone use is occurring in their classrooms, but those individual answers need a larger context and independent verification. A recent survey of 269 college students representing 21 majors from 36 different courses, equally distributed between first-year students, sophomores, juniors, and seniors, offers this kind of benchmarking data. This student cohort answered 26 questions that inquired about their use of cell phones as well as their observations regarding the cell phone use of their peers.

Virtually all the students (99 percent) reported that they had cell phones, and 97 percent said that they used their phones for text messaging. Another significant majority (95 percent) said they brought their phones to class every day, and 91 percent reported that they set their phones to vibrate. Only 9 percent said that they turned their phones off.

As for their use of cell phones, 97 percent said they sent or received text messages while waiting for class to begin, and 92 percent admitted that they had sent or received a text message during class. Thirty percent reported that they send and receive messages every day in class. Virtually all these students (97 percent) indicated that they had seen texting being done by other students in the classroom.

However, these students did not feel that their instructors know that they are texting. Almost half of them "indicated that it is easy to text in class without the instructor being aware." (p. 4) One survey question asked students to complete this statement: "If college instructors only knew _____ about text messaging in the classroom, they would be shocked."

The most common student response, offered by 54 percent of the students, was that teachers would be shocked if they knew how much texting was occurring in class. Obviously, class size influences the extent of texting, or at least student perceptions of how easy it is to text without the teacher knowing.

Did students in this survey report that they were using their cell phones to cheat? Ten percent did indicate that they had sent or received a text message during an exam, with 9 percent saying it was easy to text during exams. Interestingly, 33 percent of students in the sample chose not to answer this question. The authors note, "Failure to answer could be seen as a reflection of the respondents' desire to either not risk self-incrimination, or to not reveal to faculty that texting during an exam is a possibility." (p. 4)

Students in this cohort didn't feel that texting caused serious problems in the classroom. They did understand that the person texting is distracted and maybe distracts a few students sitting nearby, but these students were reluctant to support a policy that forbids the use of cell phones.

More than 64 percent believed students should be allowed to keep their cell phones on as long as they are placed on vibrate. Fewer than 1 percent said that cell phones should not be permitted in the classroom under any circumstances. About one-third reported that it was easier to text in a class if the professor had no policy against cell phones or appeared to be laid-back and relaxed about their use.

When asked about cell phone policies that work, students didn't offer much in the way of concrete suggestions beyond being able to use them as long as they didn't disturb others. Faculty policies described in the article include confiscating any phone that rings or phones that are being used for texting. Some professors answer phones that ring in class. If a student is observed texting, some professors count that student as absent for the day.

Given the pervasiveness of cell phones and the acceptability of their use almost anywhere these days, it's difficult to imagine successfully enforcing almost any policy in the classroom and still having time left to teach. This article includes an appendix that contains the questions used in the survey.

The use of cell phones and texting in your classes could be sensibly addressed by asking your students to respond to these questions. That way, you'd know for sure how much texting is happening, and you'd have something concrete on the topic to discuss with students. The article also contains references to several studies documenting how texting interferes with and compromises learning.

Reference: Tindell, D.R., and Bohlander, R.W. (2012). "The use and abuse of cell phones and text messaging in the classroom: A survey of college students." *College Teaching*, 60 (1), 1–9.

Reprinted from *The Teaching Professor*, 26.3 (2012): 5.

Motivation: Intrinsic, Extrinsic, or More

By Maryellen Weimer, Penn State Berks, Pennsylvania

Motivation—there are two kinds: intrinsic, which involves doing something because we want to do it, and extrinsic, which is doing something because we have to do it. A negative relationship exists between the two. Extrinsic motivation undermines intrinsic motivation. Students won't be attending class because they want to if attending class is required.

As a result of this negative relationship, students don't have much intrinsic motivation, because it's been beaten out of them by most extrinsic educational experiences. And that's a nutshell version of how most teachers understand motivation.

Is that all there is to it? Steven Reiss doesn't think so, and he has done lots of research that supports his view. But first he goes after the intrinsic-extrinsic dualism, which he says fails on three counts: construct validity, measurement reliability, and experimental control. Starting with construct validity, Reiss writes, "The distinction between intrinsic and extrinsic motivation is invalid ... because motives cannot be divided into just two categories. ... Human motives are too diverse to fall into just two categories." (p. 152)

He then explains the measurement problems and experimental control issues. The research that demonstrates an undermining effect (that extrinsic motivation diminishes intrinsic motivation) is almost entirely based on single-trial studies conducted in lab settings. "Consequently, this literature says little about real-world, long-term rewards such as grades and pay." (p. 154) If the empirical arguments are of interest, they are more fully explained in the article.

Reiss proposes a multifaceted theory of motivation. In his research he identified 16 distinct universal reinforcements that he developed into an assessment tool called the Reiss Motivation Profile. "Everybody is motivated by the 16 universal reinforcements, but not in the same way. Individuals show reliable individual differences in how they prioritize these 16 reinforcements." (pp. 154–155)

These 16 reinforcements are listed in the article, and they include the following motivations (among others): eating, the desire for food; curiosity, the desire for understanding; independence, the desire for self-reliance; social contact, the desire for peer companionship; and vengeance, the desire to confront those who offend.

To show the inadequacy of the intrinsic-extrinsic dualism, Reiss suggests giving students a list of motives like those on the profile and then asking students to rank their importance. "Doing this tends to show the extraordinary individuality of how people prioritize motives." (p. 155) Some students rank money and status very high; others list the desire for social justice as much more motivating than money.

Reiss asks whether "the information contained [on the various student lists] could possibly be captured by dualism, which has only two categories or kinds of motives. Dualism does not state what moves us; it does not show how we differ as individuals." (p. 155)

Reiss says that researchers have moved beyond the dualistic study of intrinsic and extrinsic motivation. They see motivation as multifaceted, and he challenges teachers to move forward in their thinking as well. Students in our classrooms do and don't do things in response to a variety of motives. It's more complicated than we tend to think, but this new understanding of motivation better explains how it works and can be harnessed in the interest of learning.

Reference: Reiss, S. (2012). "Intrinsic and extrinsic motivation." *Teaching of Psychology, 39* (2), 152–156.

Reprinted from *The Teaching Professor,* 26.5 (2012): 3.

Last Class:
Critical Course Component

By Vianne Timmons and Brian D. Wagner, University of Prince Edward Island, Canada

There has been significant and well-deserved attention paid to the first class. This class is critical in setting the tone and expectations of the course. Unfortunately, the same amount of attention has not been paid to the **last class**. To us, this class is as important as the first. It is the class where the professor has an opportunity to celebrate the learning of the students. Unfortunately, this day is usually saved for final exam review; finishing up projects; or dealing with logistical details such as date, time, and location of the final or where to pick up graded term papers. The course ends with a whimper instead of a bang.

We want to challenge professors to make better use of what this last day affords. We have some suggestions, but the intent of this article is not to prescribe a structure for the last class but rather to encourage faculty to think about how they might still review, if need be, but also how they might use the day to celebrate and reflect with students.

It can be helpful to connect the first and last classes. In our first class we have the students fill out expectation cards for the course. Students write out their own expectations and objectives for the course on index cards that we provide. We mix up the cards and have each student read one card (presumably not their own) either to the entire class (if the number is under 40) or to each other in groups of five.

We then compare their course objectives and expectations with our own and discuss similarities and differences. The cards are then gathered and used again in the last class as part of a review exercise. Again, we have each student read a card, and after each one we discuss whether the expectations stated were in fact met or whether this would be an area for further study or subsequent classes (sometimes we have a short discussion of the topic at that time).

The last class can be structured in many ways. In addition to the review exercise based on expectation cards, we regularly have the students group to review and discuss the course content based on the syllabus. We may have them discuss practice exam questions we provide or have them develop potential exam questions.

It is an interactive class, with the students taking ownership. A review session structured like this can include a time when students share their most significant learning in the course. What they report learning adds another dimension to the review process.

Having students share what they have learned leads naturally to a celebration of that learning. This can be done in many ways. For example, the professor can provide treats, show an inspirational video, play music, or have a guest speaker—perhaps a student who took the course a number of years ago and who can reflect on important "learnings" then and now.

The last class should be one of the most important classes. It is an opportunity to bring closure to the course in a way students will remember. The class can review the course and celebrate learning. What happens on that last day gives professors a unique opportunity to gauge the success of the course. Students can offer useful feedback for the next time this or a related course is taught.

We want our students to use their learning to contribute something to society. They may not remember course content in 20 years, but maybe they will be more critical in their thinking, challenge social norms, be respectful of difference, and influence others to do the same. Parker Palmer writes in *The Courage to Teach*, "What we teach will never 'take' unless it connects with the inward, living core of our students' lives, with our students' inward teaching." (p. 31) We want our "teaching to take"; used effectively, the last class can help us achieve this.

Reprinted from *The Teaching Professor*, 21.1 (2007): 2.

About the Editor and Contributors

About Maryellen Weimer, Ph.D.

Maryellen Weimer, Ph.D., created *The Teaching Professor* newsletter in 1987 and is its editor. She is a professor emerita of Teaching and Learning at Penn State Berks and won Penn State's Milton S. Eisenhower award for distinguished teaching in 2005. She has published several books, including: *Learner-Centered Teaching: Five Key Changes to Practice* (Jossey-Bass, 2013), *Inspired College Teaching: A Career-Long Resource for Professional Growth* (Jossey-Bass, 2010), *Enhancing Scholarly Work on Teaching and Learning: Professional Literature that Makes a Difference* (Jossey-Bass, 2006).

About Alice Cassidy, Ph.D.

Alice Cassidy, Ph.D., is the author of the foreword for this collection. For 15 years, she held leadership roles at the University of British Columbia's campus-wide Centre for Teaching and Academic Growth (TAG) and at the Institute for the Scholarship of Teaching and Learning (ISoTL). She has taught science and education undergraduate and graduate courses and coordinates the 3M National Student Fellowships at the Society for Teaching and Learning in Higher Education (STLHE). Alice has led teaching and learning seminars for instructors at post-secondary institutions in Canada, China and the US.

Contributors

Sandra Allen, Columbia College Chicago, Illinois
Carl B. Bridges, Johnson Bible College, Tennessee
Kevin Brown, Lee University, Tennessee
Edward H. Burtt, Jr., Ohio Wesleyan University, Ohio
Mary C. Clement, Berry College, Georgia
Jami Cotler, Siena College, New York
Roxanne Cullen, Ferris State University, Michigan
Rob Dornsife, Creighton University, Nebraska
Jason Ebbeling, Menlo College, California,
Karen Eifler, University of Portland, Oregon
Natasha Flowers, Indiana University-Purdue University Indianapolis, Indiana
Jeff Fox, Brigham Young University, Utah
Jim Guinee, University of Central Arkansas
Peter J. Kakela, Michigan State University, Michigan

Patricia Kohler-Evans, University of Central Arkansas, Arkansas
Joe Kreizinger, Northwest Missouri State University, Missouri
Sarah M. Leupen , Ohio Wesleyan University, Ohio
Ken MacMillan, University of Calgary, Alberta, Canada
Lori Norin, University of Arkansas—Fort Smith, Arkansas
Christy Price, Dalton State College, Georgia
E. Shelley Reid, George Mason University, Virginia
Elayne Shapiro, University of Portland, Oregon
Angie Thompson, St. Francis Xavier University, Nova Scotia, Canada
Vianne Timmons , University of Prince Edward Island, Canada
Joseph W. Trefzger, Illinois State University, Illinois
Brian Van Brunt, Western Kentucky University, Kentucky
Patti Vitale, Brown School, New York
Brian D. Wagner, University of Prince Edward Island, Canada
Tom Walton, University of Arkansas—Fort Smith, Arkansas
Katherine Whatley, Berry College, Georgia
Robert Yoder, Siena College, New York

Additional Resources

If you enjoyed this e-book, *The Teaching Professor* has additional resources for you:

Book
Grading Strategies for the College Classroom: A Collection of Articles for Faculty (http://amzn.to/15RhFLX)
This book provides insights into managing the complicated task of assigning a simple letter to a semester's work. It's a must-read for any faculty member seeking to understand how to use assessment to measure and enhance performance.

Free Resources
- Subscribe to *Faculty Focus (facultyfocus.com)* — An e-newsletter on effective teaching strategies for the college classroom, featuring a weekly blog post from Maryellen Weimer, Ph.D.
- Join *The Teaching Professor*'s LinkedIn Group *(http://linkd.in/1496hsq)*
- Like *The Teaching Professor* on Facebook *(facebook.com/TeachingProfessor)*
- Follow *The Teaching Professor* on Twitter *(@teachprof)*

Paid Resources
The Teaching Professor **Newsletter** *(teachingprofessor.com/newsletter)*
All articles in this e-book are from past editions of this newsletter. Published ten times a year, *The Teaching Professor* newsletter features ideas, insights, and best pedagogical practices written for and by educators who are passionate about teaching. Edited by Maryellen Weimer, Ph.D.

The Teaching Professor **Conference** *(teachingprofessor.com/conferences)*
This annual event provides an opportunity to learn effective pedagogical techniques, hear from leading teaching experts, and interact with colleagues committed to teaching and learning excellence.

(Continued on page 108)

The Teaching Professor Technology Conference
(teachingprofessor.com/conferences)
This conference examines the technologies that are changing the way teachers teach and students learn, while giving special emphasis to the pedagogically effective ways you can harness these new technologies in your courses and on your campus.

The Teaching Professor Workshops *(teachingprofessor.com/workshops)*
These are two-day "hands-on" learning events. At the end of the workshop, you will leave with a product or process that you can implement immediately. Topics include: learner-centered course design, grading, and blended learning.

***

Made in the USA
Lexington, KY
13 December 2013